Esse
Gui
Chakras

Essential Guide to Chakras

Swami Saradananda

WATKINS
Sharing Wisdom Since 1893

The Essential Guide to Chakras
Swami Saradananda

This edition first published in the USA in
2018 by Watkins, an imprint of
Watkins Media Limited
Unit 11, Shepperton House, 83–93
Shepperton Road
London N1 3DF

enquiries@watkinspublishing.com

Managing Editor: Sandra Rigby
Senior Editor: Fiona Robertson
Editor: Jo Godfrey Wood
Cover Design: Georgina Hewitt
Layout: Luana Gobbo
Picture Research: Julia Ruxton
Production: Ben Goodwin
Commissioned Artwork: Gary Walton
Commissioned Photography: Jules Selmes

A CIP record for this book is available from
the British Library.

ISBN: 978-1-78678-202-1

10 9 8 7 6 5 4 3 2

Typeset in Gill Sans and Rue Display
Colour reproduction by Colourscan
Printed in China

Publisher's note: The information in this
book is not intended as a substitute for
professional medical advice and treatment.
If you are pregnant or are suffering from
any medical conditions or health problems,
it is recommended that you consult a
medical professional before following any
of the advice or practice in this book.
Watkins Media Limited, or any other
persons who have been involved in
working on this publication, cannot
accept responsibility for any injuries or
damage incurred as a result of following
the information, exercises or therapeutic
techniques contained in this book.

www.watkinspublishing.com

Contents

CHAPTER ONE
Introducing Chakra Energy 6

CHAPTER TWO
Overcoming Blockages to
    Working with Chakras 32

CHAPTER THREE
Basic Techniques of Chakra
    Work 54

CHAPTER FOUR
The Muladhara Chakra 76

CHAPTER FIVE
The Swadhisthana Chakra
    100

CHAPTER SIX
The Manipura Chakra 122

CHAPTER SEVEN
The Anahata Chakra 144

CHAPTER EIGHT
The Vishuddha Chakra 166

CHAPTER NINE
The Ajna Chakra 188

CHAPTER TEN
The Sahasrara Chakra 210

CHAPTER ELEVEN
Chakra Inter-relationships
    232

CHAPTER TWELVE
Protection During Energetic
    Work 254

Further Reading 276

Glossary 277

Index 281

Acknowledgments 288

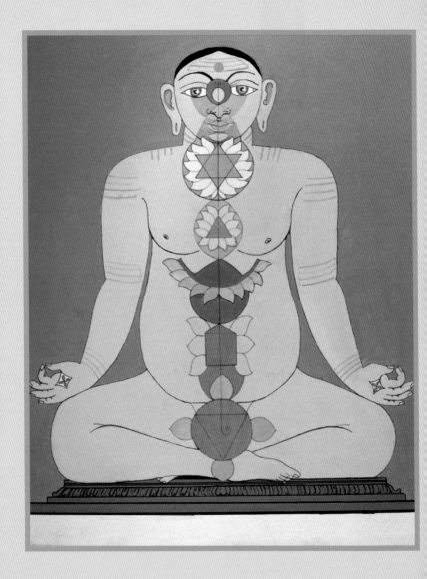

CHAPTER ONE

Introducing Chakra Energy

"The chakras or force-centres are points of
connection in which energy flows from one
vehicle or body of a man to another."

C.W. Leadbeater, *The Chakras*

Chakras: An Overview

Chakras are major centres of radiant power within your subtle body. There are seven of them, representing the energetic intersection between physical matter and your consciousness. Each of your chakras is an antenna that is constantly receiving and transmitting energy. How smoothly your chakras function determines how fully you inhabit your body, how successful you are in your relationships and how much inner peace you enjoy.

Working with your chakras can help you to restore and enhance your energy flow. The practices in this book are designed to help you keep your life in balance, whatever the complications of daily existence. With regular practice you may find that you are able to tap into the vast potential of the psycho-spiritual energy known as kundalini that lies dormant in your lower chakras.

I don't advise you to read through this book in a single sitting, but I do suggest that you begin by practising the introductory meditations on pages 72–5. These exercises will enable you to actually experience the energy centres that we call chakras. They will help you to connect with them within your own body, so that you no longer think of them as purely philosophical concepts. You will be better able to understand where your particular weaknesses may lie. Also, you will become more aware of blockages, distortions of energy and any other problems on which you might want to work.

Reading the three introductory chapters (pages 8–75) before you start on the chakra chapters (pages 76–231) will greatly enhance your understanding of the chakras themselves. The main part of the book is the seven chapters that each deal with a specific chakra. Each chapter begins with an introduction to the particular chakra and the benefits of working with it. After a discussion of the symbolic elements and iconography of the chakra, there is a meditation on the yantra (stylized diagram) of the chakra. This is followed by a look at possible reasons why a specific chakra might be out of balance and/or blocked, and ideas for rebalancing it. Each chapter ends with suggestions for practice: there are two meditations and yoga postures that work with each chakra.

The penultimate chapter (pages 232–53) looks at how the chakras work with each other, outlining some of the energetic relationships in your life that might benefit from your chakra work. And the final chapter (pages 254–75) talks about how to shield yourself from negative influences while you are working energetically. This book is intended as a basic introduction to chakras.

Centres of subtle energy in the astral body, the seven major chakras strongly influence your physical body and every aspect of consciousness.

Sahasrara,
or crown, chakra

Ajna,
or brow, chakra

Vishuddha,
or throat, chakra

Anahata,
or heart, chakra

Manipura,
or solar plexus, chakra

Swadhisthana,
or sacral, chakra

Muladhara,
or root, chakra

Prana and Nadis

The three bodies

To better understand the role of the chakras, it may be helpful for you to have a look at the yoga theory that postulates a model of three bodies: physical, astral and causal. Each of these bodies is more subtle in nature than the previous one. The most concrete of the three is the body with which you are most familiar, and refer to as "my body" in everyday language. This is your physical body, which is made up of the food that you eat. It is the body that you were born into and which you have seen grow and change. As you get older your physical body will begin to break down and eventually it will die. After death your physical body will decay and its components will return to the cycle of nature.

The second body, your astral body, includes all your qualities and attributes that are non-physical in nature. For example, although you might experience love in the region of your heart, your emotions themselves are not physical things. They strongly affect your physical body, but have their seat in your astral body – as do your mind, your intellect and your prana (see page 13).

The third body, which yogis refer to as the "seed" or "causal" body, contains the subtle kernels that germinate to produce your life. This is the storehouse of your karma and of all the subtle impressions that you take in – during your past lives as well as the present one. This body contains the seeds that determine your talents and aptitudes, your emotional make-up and even your physical appearance.

Your true essence, which is pure consciousness, is beyond the illusion of all of these three bodies. Trying to understand and identify with the true Self is the goal of all yoga practices.

Causal body

Astral body

Physical body

According to yoga philosophy, there is much more to life than just the physical elements that make up the physical body.

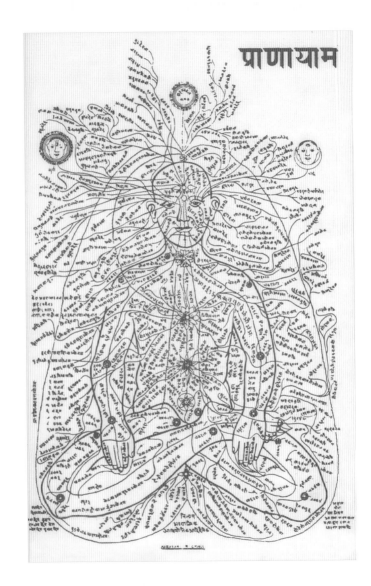

Prana

The first layer of your astral body serves as the interface between your physical body and your more subtle essence. This layer has many names, including the aura, the etheric double and the bio-magnetic field. It approximates your physical body, but it is energetic in its nature, instead of being made up of physical elements.

The word "prana", which is usually interpreted as "life force" or "vital energy", cannot actually be effectively translated into English, or into any other Western language, because until very recently the concept did not exist in Western culture. The Chinese word "chi" (as in tai *chi*) or the Japanese word "ki" (as in a*kido* or rei*ki*) are exact translations.

People who practise acupuncture, reflexology, shiatsu and most of the martial arts are working with prana. Prana is not physical in nature, but flows through your physical body, interpenetrating it as water fills a sponge. Prana is quite different from the "electricity" that moves through your nervous system.

Nadis

Prana flows through the physical body in subtle channels known as "nadis". An acupuncture chart is a representation of the nadis. In Sanskrit, the word "nadi" actually means the riverbed that contains the water or the channel through which the river flows. Approximately 72,000 nadis, referred to as "meridians" in acupuncture, make up the subtle wiring of your pranic sheath.

Another way to understand the concepts of nadis and prana would be to visualize the nadis as a road system that enables traffic (prana) to move. A junction where two or more roads meet is more likely to become blocked than a straight, uninterrupted stretch. When roads come together, there is more likelihood that a traffic jam will develop.

An ancient Indian view of the nadi network in your astral body. Nadis penetrate every aspect of your physical body, as water saturates a sponge.

Energy Centres of the Subtle Body

A chakra is any location where two or more nadis (meridians) cross; these are junctions of vibrant energy and many of the smaller chakras are used as acupuncture points. The seven "major" chakras are energetic centres located along the central nadi, which approximates your spine. The effect is rather like a telephone exchange, with many wires (nadis) coming in and going out. You could also compare the chakra system to the internet, with every part of the web connecting directly to every other part.

The word "chakra" is a bit misleading, as it is usually translated as "wheel". However, a wheel can only move forward and backward. When you want to drive your car to the right, you turn the wheels in that direction and then move forward. In fact, each chakra is more like a multi-dimensional ball of radiant energy. It is a vortex or an energetic toroid, meaning that its movement takes place on a circular, doughnut-like axis, in a twisting motion.

Each chakra is an essential part of an energetic matrix supporting your physical body. They are conduits that conduct and transform prana (subtle energy) into material form. Proper and unrestricted flow of energy through your chakras is necessary for physical, mental and emotional good health. If chakras are not functioning properly, the associated body organs and systems will become impaired.

Each of the seven major chakras represents a particular energy frequency. When fully functional and connected, they provide incredible creative control over physical matter. Energetic flow through your chakras is largely determined by your mental state. Holding fears and misconceptions in your consciousness impedes, and even reverses, the flow of energy. By working with your chakras, you can reintroduce a full, healthy flow. The real challenge is identifying the blockages and misconceptions.

A Nepalese picture of the chakras from the 18th century, including a number of minor chakras.

The Benefits of Working with the Chakras

The traumas and challenges of daily life often pull you in opposing directions. Think of a common situation, such as getting upset with your boss: you may want to speak up, yet you are afraid to say anything. Situations such as this can cause your energy to become blocked and stagnant.

Working with your chakras can assist you in finding innovative ways to free the various aspects of your being. It can facilitate new insights for you, healthier behaviour patterns and a more rewarding lifestyle. Your chakras are energetic centres that you can use to connect more fully with other people and experience inner peace. Each one is a door that can be opened to greater energetic, psychic and spiritual knowledge. Or it can stay closed, causing you to remain within your present limitations.

When your energy is flowing smoothly through each chakra and between the chakras, you tend to look after yourself better. You possess self-confidence and can communicate your thoughts, hopes and dreams in a healthy manner. You function in a more relaxed manner, yet are more focused. Your natural immunity is increased and you are better able to deal with stress. Your intuition is enhanced and you have a clearer insight into your purpose in the world.

Chakra work involves a number of simple, yet powerful techniques that can help you to develop inner poise and keep your life in balance. These practices are most helpful when you reinforce them with regular self-analysis and bolster them with positive activities, such as a healthy diet and regular yoga practice. Chakra work can prove to be an adventure of self-discovery – and the best time to embark on your inner pilgrimage is right now!

When to work with chakra energy

If you feel spaced out or disconnected from the world around you, perhaps you need to explore working with your lower chakras for their grounding effects. But when your life seems a bit dull and you would like to experience more inspiration, you might try working with some of the higher chakras. These are also effective when you are thinking of making major changes in your life, especially ones to bring you more in line with your spiritual goals. Or you might want to work with chakra energy whenever you want to see new horizons on your inner journey through life.

A regular home practice of meditation can help to put you in tune with the working of your chakras.

Sources of Chakra Wisdom

Working with your chakras means striving toward inner peace, using various techniques to achieve a blissful and worry-free state. According to yoga philosophy, Maya (the cosmic Illusion) has caused the universe to come into being. Creation proceeds from the most subtle to the progressively more dense. First there was only pure Consciousness, from which came the Supreme Mind. Primordial space (ether) came into being and, within that, swirling gases (air) formed. Before our planet became solid it was liquid, like the molten lava of a volcano. Before it was liquid it was "fire", like the sun.

Your physical body is composed of the same five elements as everything else in the universe. At the time of your death, your body will become cold as the fire element leaves it. Your lifeless body

Chakra work can be grounding or freeing.

CHAKRA WORK FOR GROUNDING		THE CHAKRAS	THE ELEMENTS OF CREATION	CHAKRA WORK FOR FREEING
		Sahasrara	**Cosmic consciousness**	
	Matter becomes more concrete (creation)	Ajna	**Mind** – your sense of individual self	
Work in the world		Vishuddha	**Ether** – space	
		Anahata	**Air** – matter in a gaseous state	Meditation
Work out your karma		Manipura	**Fire** – physical energy, heat, light	Matter absorbed into more subtle state (liberation)
		Swadhisthana	**Water** – matter in a liquid state	
		Muladhara	**Earth** – matter in a solid state	

will bloat up as the gases leave it; it will dry up as the water leaves it; and its earth element will return to the earth as the body decomposes. Finally your body will cease to occupy space as it disintegrates completely.

The energy of each of the physical elements is represented by one of the chakras. In meditation, each element may be visualized as merging with its source, starting with the grossest and proceeding to the most subtle. The earth element of the root chakra (muladhara) is merged into its source – water. The water element of the sacral chakra (swadhisthana) is merged into its source – fire. The fire element of the solar plexus chakra (manipura) is absorbed into air. The air element of the heart chakra (anahata) is absorbed into the ether of the throat chakra (vishuddha). Ether is absorbed into the mind at the brow chakra (ajna). And finally the mind merges into the absolute consciousness of the crown chakra (sahasrara).

Working with chakras

In chakra work the macrocosm of the universe is a model for the microcosm of your own being. Chakra work aims at integrating every aspect of your body, mind and spirit by providing you with the grounding to work in the world.

There are times when you may feel the need for more stability. Working with the lower chakras gives you a firm foundation in your life and practice. You may want to start here and then return to work with the lower chakras whenever you need more grounding, for example after you have returned from travelling. It can also be helpful when you have gone through a major upset, such as a divorce or job loss. By working with the lower chakras, you enhance your stability in life. Your stability follows the path of creation.

Conversely, at other times, your life may seem to be a bit stuck. This is the time to work with your higher chakras, preferably from the firm foundation that you have created. This can give you a greater sense of liberation and freedom in your life.

Different approaches to the chakras

The concept of the chakra system is an integral part of hatha yoga practice. Although there are similar concepts of prana (chi or ki) and nadis (meridians) in Taoist teachings, there is very little about the seven major energy centres that are referred to as the chakras. This may be because the Chinese teachings deal mainly with the energetic principles as they relate to health, whereas the yoga teachings are focused on the use of the energetic body for spiritual enlightenment as well.

We find mention of subtle energy centres in the Tibetan Bonpo and Mayan religions, and also in the Inca, Cherokee (Native American), Egyptian and African traditions. Some modern writers have equated the ancient chakra wisdom of yoga with the Christian sacraments and also with the Kabbalah's Tree of Life.

In this book we focus mainly on the yoga model of chakras, which recognizes that they do not exist in a physical sense; they are purely energetic in nature and are intimately linked and anchored to different points in your physical body. The chakras filter all the events of your daily life, as well as your dreams, fears, hopes, desires, regrets, thoughts and communication. They are the ultimate devices by which you store, sort and retrieve the vast variety of data that your mind and body are constantly receiving.

In Greek and Roman mythology, Hermes/ Mercury, the messenger of the gods, carries the caduceus, a short staff entwined by two serpents and sometimes topped by wings. Serpents are a traditional symbol of rebirth. In yoga tradition, the caduceus may be seen as a picture of the three main nadis. The ida and pingala criss-cross over the sushumna (the central nadi on which the chakras are located) until they join at the ajna, or brow, chakra, which looks like a winged seed.

Chakra theory is an essential aspect of hatha yoga.

The Chakras Move West

The concept of the chakras and associated Eastern teachings took many centuries to travel to the West and take root in so-called New Age philosophy. Perhaps the earliest (surviving) book on chakras is the *Sat-Cakra-Nirupana*. It is believed to have been written more than 500 years ago in Sanskrit by a Bengali yogi named Purnananda. This highly regarded book has been the subject of numerous commentaries.

Sir John Woodroffe, who wrote under the pen name Arthur Avalon, was one of the first to bring the concept of chakras to the West. He translated the *Sat-Cakra-Nirupana* and the *Padaka-Pancakam* into English. These texts, along with his own commentary, formed the basis of his famous book, *The Serpent Power*, which was first published in 1919. Woodroffe's book is extremely detailed and complex; his ideas were developed into what is the predominant Western view of the chakras by members of the Theosophical Society. Their writings put chakra terminology into modern language.

Rudolf Steiner, founder of Anthroposophy, wrote that the chakra system is constantly evolving, is very different for modern people from what it was in ancient times, and will be radically different in the future. *How to Know Higher Worlds* (1904) gives instructions for chakra work that are more like life disciplines than exercises.

In his 1927 book, *The Chakras*, C.W. Leadbeater, a member of the

Rudolf Steiner wrote more than 300 books on esoteric subjects, including the chakras.

Carl Jung, the founder of analytical psychology, encouraged scientific exploration of the chakras.

Theosophical Society, gives an analysis of the chakras that, for the most part, is the result of his own meditations and clairvoyant insights. Leadbeater is one of the first writers to assign specific colours to the chakras and this idea, which is not present in any ancient traditions, caught on with many New Age writers and practitioners.

In 1932, psychoanalyst Carl Jung presented a series of talks on kundalini yoga to the Psychological Club in Zurich. The seminar is widely regarded as a milestone in the psychological understanding of the chakras, and Eastern thought in general. Jung saw the chakra system as a model for the development of higher consciousness, and he interpreted its symbols in terms of the process of the development of the individual.

Gopi Krishna, the Indian yogi, teacher and writer, also popularized kundalini among Western readers. As he says in his book *Kundalini – The Secret of Yoga*, his writings attempt to bring the ancient concepts in line with "the enormous advances made in psychology, physiology and other branches of knowledge relevant to this subject".

Writers continue to explore the relevance of the chakras to our lives. In his 1988 book *Chakras*, Indian scholar and Tantra practitioner Harish Johari reintroduces the classical principles of the chakras, as well as their practical applications in modern life. In *Anatomy of Spirit*, her breakthrough book of 1996, the medical intuitive Caroline Myss compares the chakra system with the Tree of Life of the Kabbalah, as well as with the seven Christian Sacraments. In *Wheels of Life* (1987) and in her other books, Anodea Judith takes a practical and psychological approach. And my 2008 book *Chakra Meditation* integrates chakra work with yoga and meditation practice.

Kundalini

The word "kundalini" comes from the Sanskrit word "kundala", meaning "coiled". This untapped energy is symbolized by a snake. In Indian tradition, snakes represent wisdom and eternal life. In her dormant state, Kundalini lies coiled three and a half times around a Siva lingam (representing the formless) in the muladhara chakra.

Kundalini is the infinite spiritual potential that lies dormant within you. When this latent power becomes active, your thoughts and consciousness become especially inspired and powerful. In symbolic terms, you have "awakened the sleeping goddess". When the vast quiescent energy of kundalini is released, it may be likened to the floodgates of a dam being opened. Once awakened, kundalini manifests as high-voltage energy that causes you to experience a state of heightened awareness and increased capabilities.

Awakening kundalini

All the nadis (meridians), especially the central sushumna nadi, need to be purified and strengthened so that the kundalini energy can flow without overloading your system. Most yoga texts warn you not to attempt to raise the kundalini too early. When your system is ready, a natural awakening will occur.

Practices that increase the likelihood that you will awaken your kundalini include physical and mental purifications, such as eating a pure diet, fasting and doing kriyas (yoga cleansing exercises, see page 36). Also recommended are concentration on the chakras, karma yoga (selfless service) and a powerful longing to achieve direct connection with divine energies. Breathing exercises also assist the flow of kundalini, including the yoga practice of pranayama,

This sculpture of a Siva lingam, protected here by a seven-hooded serpent, represents the mystical potential of kundalini energy.

This picture of the chakras also shows the major nadis known as the ida, pingala and sushumna (central nadi).

rebirthing and holodynamic breathing. Use of mudras (energetic seals) and bandhas (energy locks) are described on pages 30–31. Chanting mantras can open the channels to prepare the way for increased kundalini energy or clear blockages in the chakras.

The stronger and more purified your system is, the less likely it will be for you to have negative or painful experiences during kundalini awakening (see box opposite). When your physical and astral bodies are strengthened and purified, and the energy flowing through each chakra is balanced, awakened kundalini energy can bring you great joy and an awareness of higher realms of existence. If you have prepared yourself properly, this gently rising current of energy activates, purifies and empowers all levels of consciousness.

SENSATIONS OF KUNDALINI AWAKENING

- Hot and/or ice-cold currents moving up and down your spine
- Sensations as though a snake is wriggling up your spine or tingling sensations in your spine, abdomen, neck and head
- Pains that move around your body, without stress in your joints or muscles
- Stiffness in your neck, sometimes accompanied by headaches
- Unusual vibrations and feelings of restlessness in your arms, hands, legs and feet
- Increased rates of pulse and breathing
- Hypersensitivity to sound, light and smells
- The development of psychic/paranormal abilities, known in Sanskrit as "siddhis"
- Visions of devas, angels, saints, sages and celestial musicians
- Sensations of rotating or floating in the air. If this is frightening, practise grounding visualizations, picturing yourself as firmly rooted in the ground or sending down roots.
- "Hearing" mystical sounds, such as the tinkling of wind chimes, ringing bells, blowing conch shells, the playing of a lute or cymbals, flute music (mostly in the early morning), the beating of a drum, the rumble of distant thunder
- Sleeplessness – or unusual amounts of energy
- Desire for solitude
- Intense joy and bliss. If your kundalini has been raised prematurely, these highs may alternate with periods of deep depression.
- Flashes of inspiration and innovative ideas

The Granthis

One way of perceiving your body is using the analogy of a building that is wired for a certain amount of energy. If you turn on too many appliances, the circuit breaker will shut off the power to protect the building from burning down. In the anatomy of your astral body, the circuit breaker is a "granthi"; a term often translated as a "knot".

You have three energetic "knots" that shield you from premature or excessive release of kundalini energy. When your nadis (meridians) have been purified and strengthened sufficiently to handle the increased surge of energy, each granthi will open to allow the released potential to rise. The granthis are not blockages; they are protective mechanisms that prevent the excessive flow of prana along the central nadi. They stop the kundalini energy from shooting through your body before you are ready and able to deal with it.

Untying the knots

These three psychic knots are the brahma granthi, the vishnu granthi and the rudra granthi. The brahma granthi, in the muladhara chakra, represents your attachment to stability, inertia and your misidentification with your physical body. In order for this knot to open, you must give up the expectation that there is any lasting happiness to be found in any physical or psychological experience.

The vishnu granthi, in the anahata chakra, represents attachment to action, ambition and passion. For this to open, you need to practise forgiveness. It is especially important that you are able to forgive yourself.

The rudra granthi, in your ajna chakra, is connected with your attachment to your intellectual powers and to self-image. In order for this knot to open, you need to overcome the dictates of your ego.

The granthis (knots) that prevent release of kundalini energy are located in the ajna, anahata and muladhara chakras.

Mudras and Bandhas

The seven major chakras of your subtle body can be seen as powerful antennae that are constantly receiving and transmitting energy. To enable you to work with them more effectively many yoga techniques employ bandhas that "lock" your subtle energy into specific channels, and mudras that help you to "seal" your energy.

Although "bandha" is usually translated as "lock", it also means to tie, to control, to hold, to join and to contract. In breathing exercises "bandha" usually refers to the muscular contractions that assist you in focusing your energy.

Mudras are hand, head and postural positions that seal the psychic energies into specific channels. They assist you in establishing a direct link between your physical and astral bodies. Mudras are like switches that can create particular flows of energy within your body. They are powerful tools to help you redirect your prana and to awaken your kundalini.

The purpose of mudras and bandhas is the purification of the mental and physical bodies. They are excellent for people who want to achieve inner peace, but have trouble controlling their senses.

Jalandhara bandha

The most commonly used bandha is jalandhara (neck lock), which works with one of your most important acupressure areas. In Sanskrit, the word "jala" means net or network. It refers to your spine and the network of nerves at your neck, which connects to your brain. "Dhara" denotes the upward pull.

Jalandhara bandha exerts an upward pull on your spinal cord and on your nerve centres, which in turn work on your brain. By applying jalandhara bandha, you bring your lungs and cardiovascular system more easily under your conscious control. You also calm your heartbeat, establishing a strong and steady rhythm.

Jalandhara bandha is the chin lock that helps you to focus your mind and awaken the dormant kundalini energy.

In this exercise, you bring the top of your tongue up flat against the roof of your mouth. Then swallow so that your tongue slides back as far as possible. Keeping your back straight, bend your neck and bring your chin down to rest in the jugular notch (the central point of your collar bones).

The purpose of jalandhara bandha is to awaken and localize the subtle energies within your physical and astral bodies. The best preliminary practice of jalandhara bandha is the shoulderstand (see page 184). Practise this first. Once you have mastered the shoulderstand, consult a knowledgeable yoga teacher about using the jalandhara bandha to augment your other yoga practices.

CHAPTER TWO

Overcoming Blockages to Working with Chakras

"One should practise pranayama
with a pure mind until the central nadi is
free from all impurities."

Hatha Yoga Pradipika, 2.6

Physical blockages

If you find it difficult to balance the energy of your chakras, perhaps you haven't released the deep blockages within your nadis (meridians). Blockages are points where the movement of your subtle energy meets resistance – and this chapter explores the many reasons for the existence of these stumbling blocks to your progress. They may be the result of physical conditions, distorted energetic patterns, erroneous beliefs that you hold, emotional imbalances and/ or spiritual misconceptions.

It is often the case that physical problems prevent you from making optimal use of your prana. The blockage may be the result of an injury (such as a broken leg), an ailment (such as a cold, sore throat or headache), a disease (such as diabetes) or an addiction to an unhealthy physical substance. Being tired may block your physical as well as your mental capacities; exhaustion usually distorts your perspective and inhibits your effective functioning.

If you block a river by throwing waste into it, its flow is reduced. Similarly, if your body is filled with physical toxins, the flow of prana is inhibited. Physical blocks can affect your feelings, causing you to be bad-tempered or impatient and they may also impede your spiritual life by causing you to devote more time and attention to your physical condition.

It is probably a good idea to make clearing physical blockages your first priority. This may be as simple as making sure that you get enough rest and good, nutritious food, or you may need to have some form of treatment. Clearing physical blockages may involve changing your belief system, so that you can accept a type of therapy that you had previously rejected. It may also entail being able to accept and act on higher guidance.

To understand potential impasses to the energy-flows through your chakras, a helpful analogy is the electrical concept of "resistance". Pure copper wires are an excellent conductor of electricity. However, if the wiring is frayed or there are impurities mixed in with the copper, the flow along the wires is reduced. Similarly, the greater the impurities within your physical body, the more resistance there will be.

Impurities and physical blockages to the flow of prana can be alleviated by practising asanas, kriya, pranayama, a pure and healthy diet and fasting. These methods are described on the next page.

When a river is unblocked and free from impurities, the flow of the water is healthy and strong. The same is true when your nadis are free from toxins.

Asanas

In addition to enhancing your flexibility, yoga postures massage your internal organs and tone your endocrine system. Asanas differ from most other forms of physical exercise in that they oppose violent movements and they are not likely to produce large quantities of lactic acid in your muscles. They release blocked-up energy so that you tend to feel more energetic after your practice; you aren't tired, as you are after other forms of exercise.

Kriyas

Yoga cleansing exercises assist nature in removing waste products from your physical body and your nadis. These practices speed up the detoxification process greatly. In addition to bathing and brushing your teeth, you may want to practise neti (see box, opposite).

Pranayama

Your physical breath is viewed as the outward manifestation of your prana; yoga breathing (pranayama) exercises begin by enabling you to control the motion of your lungs. They assist you in releasing physical toxins and cleansing the physical body.

Pure and healthy diet

If your food is heavy or impure, the flow of your prana becomes lethargic. If your diet tends toward more stimulating foods, it makes your energy jumpy and erratic. It is probably best to keep your diet as simple, light and nutritious as possible. This encourages a healthy body, a calm mind and an unblocked flow of prana through the nadis.

Fasting

This permits your digestive system to rest while ridding your body of toxins. It cleanses and enhances the flow of prana. Even a one-day fast makes your body feel lighter. You use the energy that it usually directs toward digestion to repair and heal your physical body.

Neti is an excellent method to cleanse your nasal passages and sinus cavities of pollution, dust, pollen and excess mucus. It is useful for everyone, but especially if you suffer from asthma, allergies and other respiratory problems. You can do this simple hygienic practice daily – preferably each morning just after you have brushed your teeth.

You will need:

- A small neti pot with a spout. These are available from most health-food shops, as well as many pharmacies and chemists.
- A cup or so of lukewarm water
- ½ teaspoon of fine sea salt

Before practising neti, fill the neti pot with the lukewarm water. Stir in the salt until it has dissolved.

1 Leaning over a sink, inhale and hold your breath. Tighten the back of your throat as though you were about to gargle. Tilt your head to the left and pour the salt water into your right nostril. Allow gravity to drain the water out through your left nostril. Do not inhale the water.

2 Blow your nose and repeat the procedure by tilting your head to the right and pouring the water through your left nostril.

Energetic Blockages

Your prana, nadi and chakras all reside in the energetic interface between your physical and subtle bodies. This layer of your being is known by a number of names, including the pranic sheath, the energy body, the aura, the etheric double and the bio-magnetic field.

If a nadi (energetic channel) is blocked, the flow of prana to that particular region of your body will be reduced or even cut off. Without being nourished by vital energy, the part will be weakened, perhaps sickened – or it may even atrophy. For your body to be vibrantly healthy, an unimpeded flow of prana is necessary and the easiest way to achieve this is to start to work with your breath.

Also, to unblock your nadis, it is advisable to lead a lifestyle that is based on simple, healthy living and high thinking. If you are a slave to your palate or have sold yourself to sleep, you will find that your energy is being pulled in opposing directions. Also if you starve yourself or try to force yourself beyond your limits without enough rest, you will find it difficult to achieve inner peace.

Some methods of alleviating impurities and energetic blockages to the flow of prana are asanas, mouna and pranayama.

Asanas

Yoga postures work on an energetic as well as a physical level. In each position you put pressure on a different point, as if you were giving yourself a shiatsu treatment. Your asana practice helps you to release energetic blockages in the nadis. This enables prana to flow smoothly and brings it into the central channel.

To keep your energy flowing, it is advisable to establish a regular routine of yoga asanas. Active exercise, such as walking, swimming, dancing or running, will also help to keep the prana moving and assist in breaking up energetic blockages in the nadis.

Mouna

Mouna is a yoga practice that involves voluntary silence. You start by not speaking for a specific length of time. Mouna begins with physical silence, then blossoms into a state of total mental quietude. Many yoga teachers recommend that you try to practise mouna for an hour each day. Choose a time when you are not working. Do not put on the TV or play music. Use the time to observe what is going on in your mind.

Pranayama

Learning to control your breath through yoga breathing exercises (pranayama) enables you to gain conscious control of the energy moving through your subtle body. It can connect you with your suppressed emotions, help you to free yourself of your own restrictive beliefs, enhance your self-image and self-confidence, and enable you to remove energetic blockages. Alternate nostril breathing (see page 40) is one of the most common, and highly beneficial, forms of pranayama.

The shoulderstand is a useful asana for releasing blockages in the region of the upper back, neck and shoulders – and for increasing prana at the throat chakra.

Alternate nostril breathing

To release energetic blockages, the practice of alternate nostril breathing can prove very helpful. This exercise equalizes the flow of your breath. With regular practice, you will probably notice your energies becoming much more grounded. Sit in a comfortable position with your back straight. Raise your right hand and bend your index and middle fingers into the palm of your hand. You will use the thumb of your right hand to close your right nostril. Use the two end fingers (ring and little fingers) when closing your left nostril. Never swap hands, even if you are left-handed.

1 Begin by closing your right nostril with the thumb of your right hand and breathe in through the left nostril to a count of four.

2 Gently pinch both nostrils shut; hold your breath for a count of 16 (four times as long as your inhalation).

3 Release your thumb from your right nostril and breathe out through the right for a count of eight (twice the count of the inhalation), keeping your left nostril closed with your ring and little fingers.

4 With your left nostril remaining closed, breathe in through the right to a count of four.

5 Close both nostrils and hold your breath to a count of 16.

6 Release your left nostril and breathe out through the left for a count of eight, keeping the right nostril closed with your thumb. This completes one full round of alternate nostril breathing. Try to do at least 10 rounds daily.

Caution: Do not do this exercise while you are pregnant. Instead, practise without holding your breath.

Alternate nostril breathing

1

2

3

Mental–Emotional Blockages

Mental blockages tend to be negative patterns of thoughts that prevent you from reaching your full potential. They often include such beliefs as feeling that you don't deserve to be happy, ideas that you will die young (because others in your family have) or a conviction that there is no cure for whatever ails you. Often mental blocks are the result of unexpressed or insufficiently expressed emotions and feelings. They may involve early indoctrination and/or the use of recreational drugs.

Releasing mental–emotional blockages is difficult without controlling your breath, as the two are intimately connected. Notice how, when you are engaged in deep thinking or meditation, your breath is very slow. Conversely, when your mind is affected by negative emotions, it becomes irregular and unsteady. These observations demonstrate the interdependence and interaction of your prana and your mind. Such blockages often involve your five senses and your habitual mind, as well as your subconscious.

Anger

This can stem from, or create blockages at, your manipura chakra and it can do great damage to both your physical and astral bodies. Your entire nervous system may be shattered by a fit of anger. It is best to watch your mind for signs of irritability. Anger can be overcome by developing the positive counter-attitude of patience.

With repetition anger gains strength; by checking your anger you strengthen your will. The practice of meditation helps to eliminate the causes of anger; it slowly changes your values and perspectives.

Depression

This emotion can block your energy at any, or at all, of your chakras. The blockage may be the result of previous tendencies, negative

Going for a walk in the fresh air and breathing deeply can help to release your mental–emotional blockages.

company or even a cloudy day. Depression impedes the movement of prana and makes you feel lethargic. If you are feeling "down", take the time to do some yoga postures and/or breathing exercises, go for a brisk walk or sing. However, if your depression seems to be chronic, it would be best to consult your doctor or another healthcare professional.

Fear

Fear is an emotion that manifests in many forms and can cause you to feel as though all of your energy is frozen. Usually it involves blockages at your muladhara and/or swadhisthana chakras. You may experience fear of death, disease, solitude or public criticism. All forms of fear stand in the way of your freedom. You can overcome blockages caused by fear through self-enquiry, devotion to a higher cause, and the cultivation of courage (the opposite of fear).

Pre-conceived ideas

These tend to lock your energy into repetitive channels and habitual patterns of behaviour and they can create blockages at any, or all, of your chakras. Children learn so much more quickly than adults because they tend to have less previous "programming" (fewer pre-conceptions).

Develop the attitude of being a "silent witness" of your own actions. Watch yourself, even when you are engaged in habitual patterns such as brushing your teeth. Doing things consciously and mindfully helps you to remove the blockages caused by pre-conceived ideas.

Music, especially as a component of devotional practices, affects the chakras very strongly.

Some methods of alleviating mental–emotional blockages to the flow of prana are pranayama, fasting, and music and devotional practices.

Pranayama

These yoga breathing exercises help you to control consciously the movement of energy through your subtle body (see page 39).

Fasting

This brings up many emotions and helps you to release the blockages they cause. It is best to fast when you don't have to work, so that you can take the time to observe the emotions and thoughts that are coming up from your subconscious mind. Watch these movements in your consciousness, but don't permit yourself to be affected by them.

Music and devotional practices

Singing uplifting songs, playing spiritual music and engaging in devotional practices are all ways to free your emotions and release blockages. They work best when you practise them with full awareness, rather than by rote.

HOW YOUR THOUGHTS AFFECT PRANA FLOW

Remember that neither thought nor prana is in your physical body. However, according to the nature of your thoughts, prana flows to a specific region of your physical body. When your thoughts are of a dense and materialistic nature, the smooth flow of prana will be lessened, as the flow meets with too much resistance. When this happens on a regular basis, blockages will tend to form.

Intellectual Blockages

Your analytical mind may create blockages in the flow of your prana when you make decisions using poor logic – or when you base your decisions on incorrect information. These blockages are usually related to the higher chakras, such as the vishuddha and ajna. For example, you may have the impression that there is only one way to do something – or that you "have no choice" in the matter. Once the blockage is in place, it is difficult to overcome because it now seems so logical.

Doubt

When your expectations are unrealistic, you may find yourself doubting everything you do and think. Similarly, you may doubt the efficacy of regular, steady practices. Doubts such as these result in intellectual blockages to the flow of your prana. To overcome blockages cause by self-doubt, it is best to seek the company of people with similar interests. Your doubts can also be removed by regular study and philosophical enquiry.

Fault-finding and negativity

Fault-finding increases the negative attitude of your mind and does not help you to find inner peace. When your mind is engaged in activity of this sort, it tends to get stuck, causing blockages in the nadis. It is best not to dwell on the shortcomings of other people. Also, do not allow yourself to be obsessed with criticism that others direct toward you.

   If you find your mind processing and re-processing each problem and event of the day, try to develop the habit of non-attachment. You may find it helpful to visualize each negative thought as a bubble. It may seem to get bigger and bigger, but soon the bubble will pop and your mind will be free of the negative thought.

Study and the company of positive-minded people can help to release your inner turmoil, negative attitudes and habitual fault-finding.

Karma yoga

Karma yoga (selfless service) reduces negativity and gets your prana moving in positive channels. When you serve someone without self-interest, you build empathy and your heart chakra opens. This balances the "head" energy on which you were previously focusing.

Psychic powers

If you work with your chakras on a regular basis, psychic powers are likely to come as the natural outcome of your inner purification. It is important that you don't use these powers for selfish or materialistic purposes or there could be a negative reaction. Psychic powers can be strong intoxicants, causing your intellect to become cloudy.

If you have begun to work with your chakras in the hope of attaining psychic powers, it is important that you are aware of the dangers involved. Selfish motives cause attachment to such powers and produce a form of spiritual greed.

Letting go of intellectual pride

Blockages are often caused by intellectual pride. Meditation on letting go of your ego-identification and limited sense of self can help you to free up this type of blockage.

Meditation on letting go

Use your breath to release intellectual pride and anything else that might be causing energetic blockages.

❶ Sit in a comfortable position with your back straight and close your eyes. Breathe gently through your nose. Keep your awareness on your breath, but don't try to control your breath. Watch your breath. Listen to your breath. Use your breath to help you let go of stress, tensions and anxieties.

2 Breathe abdominally and deeply. As you inhale, hear your breath saying "let". As you exhale, hear your breath saying "go". Do not strain or force your breath in any way. Imagine that you are letting go of a bit of your blocked energy with each exhalation.

Conclusion

To free up the energy of your chakras from intellectual blockages, use your analytical mind to begin to discern what actually makes you happy in the long run. Carry out philosophical enquiry, but do not allow yourself to become stuck in one line of thought. Instead of trying to remove negative thoughts, perhaps you can try to cultivate the opposite: positive attitude. Also, try not to be too extreme in anything you do, because this can only disturb your inner peace.

Positive thinking and working on understanding your true essence or nature can help you to overcome blockages that are caused by an overly analytical mind – or when the energy of your ajna chakra is excessive.

A daily practice of deep breathing and meditation can help you to release some of your long-held beliefs that cause intellectual blockages.

Karmic Blockages

Karma is action. It includes the actions you have done in the past, whether in this lifetime or in past ones, and the reactions that you get from those actions. As a result of your past actions, you are enjoying (or suffering from) your present situation in life. The knowledge that you are the creator of your present situation enables you to better guide your future by removing present blockages to the flow of your prana.

To remove karmic blockages, begin by being non-judgemental, especially with yourself. Let go of the habit of constantly making comparisons; accept the fact that you are exactly where you need to be at the moment. This may involve not sweating the small stuff and being patient with those around you and with the limitations of your surroundings.

Being content in the present, while striving to improve your future life, involves a deep acceptance and understanding of the law of karma. It enables you to release the blockages that consume vast amounts of your energy with thoughts that you shouldn't have done something, or you should have done it in a different way. Learn from your mistakes and move on, without letting regrets devour you. Start noticing how your present efforts enable you to change your future.

As you go about your daily routine, without judging it, be aware of whether or not your mind is really on what you are doing. Or, is your mind stuck on recriminations about what you could/should/would have done?

Begin to accept that the past is over; you cannot change it. Even a split second after you have carried out an action, you cannot undo it. Once you have said something, it is said; you can never un-say it.

Take responsibility for your own karma. Trace every energetic blockage back to your own previous actions and attitudes. Also, whenever you feel distress of any kind, consciously choose to return to your centre of balance.

Self-less service

Perform random acts of kindness; these are selfless acts that you can carry out. Although there may be no reason for you to make another person smile, or be happier, the action helps to remove karmic blockages to your energy.

Your action can be as simple as smiling at someone, saying hello, or offering to help with something. An act of kindness isn't necessarily a grand gesture or a huge donation.

Krishna and Arjuna on the battlefield in the Bhagavad Gita *discuss karma and the need to accept responsibility for one's actions.*

Keep a journal

Keeping a journal (see page 64) can enable you to understand how your karma creates energetic blockages. Here are some questions and affirmations to use as a starting point:

- Do I live in the present moment or am I usually getting ready for something else?

- When I look at other people's lives, do I wish they were mine? Or do I tend to accept that my past actions have brought me the experience of my present situation?

- Everything I need is always there for me – even if my experience at that particular moment is a difficult one.

- When I am centred and content, my inner self remains untroubled by the stresses and strains of life.

Conclusion

Begin to develop the attitude that karmic blockages are merely "tests" on your road to self-discovery. It might also be helpful for you to envision them as lessons to be learned. When you do this, you turn each obstacle into an opportunity for self-discovery. Remember: regular, steady practice with an attitude of non-attachment is the best way to overcome blockages. Occasionally, you can give your mind a little relaxation and variety by changing your schedule of practice, but it is best if it does not stop completely. Often beginners, full of enthusiasm, hope to quickly acquire psychic powers. If you don't achieve results straight away, don't become discouraged and don't give up.

It is important that blockages are removed gradually. Sincerity, regularity and patience ensure eventual advancement.

The Tibetan Wheel of Life gives a pictorial representation of the influences of karma.

CHAPTER THREE

Basic Techniques of Chakra Work

"Undoubtedly, the mind is difficult to control and restless, but by practice, and by dispassion, it can be restrained."

Bhagavad Gita, 6.35

An Introduction to Yantras

Yantras are visual symbols that help to awaken the dormant powers that exist in a static state within your being. They help to activate your hidden potential and transform it to kinetic power.

Each picture represents the universe which, when you perceive it through your senses, appears to be made up of observable matter. In reality, matter is nothing but vibrations that your senses interpret as solid, liquid or gaseous.

A yantra is a representation of a specific energetic blueprint. It represents a matrix of geometric forms and symbolic pictures that create patterns of great power. Although yantras are usually drawn in a two-dimensional pictorial format, each one represents a multi-dimensional energy centre.

Yantras as meditation tools

Each yantra is a meditation tool that can enable you to focus on the energy of the specific chakra. Concentrating on the yantra causes an image to form in your mind with a remarkable intensity.

The literal meaning of the word yantra is "instrument" or "machine". Yantras are constructed using the principles of sacred geometry. They are symbolic representations of energy patterns and

powerful centring devices that assist you in harnessing the energy of the chakra. Like psychic sponges, yantras absorb negativity that might reside in your mind.

Yantras help to transform your existing patterns of mental behaviour into more positive habits of thought. They are often used to bring healing and to maintain health and abundance. Yantras are best understood as enhancing the potential that already exists. They cannot force something to happen that is against natural karma, but they can aid and assist in bringing about desirable outcomes.

Don't worry if you don't have a background in mathematics, even if you feel "hopeless" when it comes to geometry, the patterns represented by each yantra will work on your subconscious mind. They will help you to experience new connections between the two hemispheres of your brain.

Remember that it is important not to rush. Get to know each aspect of the picture before you advance to the next. If, at any point, your mind feels restless, start again at the outer edge of the yantra. With continued practice, you will find yourself connecting intuitively with the hidden "logic" of this geometric form that embodies the element associated with the chakra.

From left to right, the yantras of the muladhara (page 85), swadhisthana (page 109), manipura (page 131), anahata (page 153), vishuddha (page 175), ajna (page 197) and sahasrara (page 219) chakras.

Entering the universe of the yantra

If, at any point, your mind feels restless, start again at the outer edge of the yantra. When you finish your yantra meditation, it is a good idea to sit for a few minutes and note down your experiences.

① Place the picture of the yantra on a small, low table so that it is slightly below the level of your eyes when you sit for meditation.

② Sit in your preferred position for meditation. Be sure that your spine is erect, your shoulders relaxed and your chin held parallel to the ground.

③ Always start at either the "12 o'clock" position – or by looking at the outer petal in the upper right-hand corner.

④ Rotate your eyes clockwise, never in the opposite direction.

⑤ Allow your eyes to move slowly; it is important to not rush through each layer.

⑥ Notice the number and colour of the outside petals – these represent the patterns of radiant energy of the chakra. They also represent the major nadis (energy channels) that join at that specific chakra.

⑦ On each petal is written a Sanskrit letter representing a seed sound; repeat the associated mantra as you look at each letter. Do this much only for several days, until you feel you have connected fully with the energy of these peripheral mantras.

⑧ When you feel ready to advance to the next level, bring your awareness to the animal that symbolizes the elemental energy of the chakra.

⑨ Then look at the geometric form that represents the element associated with the chakra. Each geometric form has a large Sanskrit letter written in it; this is the seed sound of the element of the chakra. Each yantra always has a mantra (seed sound) associated with it. Just as your mind is a part of, yet different from, your body, so is the mantra related to the yantra. The mantra is the mind consciousness; the yantra is the form of the energy of the chakra. Within the body of each yantra – and in each petal – a monosyllabic mantra is written.

Bindu: The design of each yantra focuses your attention into the centre. Here you see a dot or "bindu". This represents the *Locus Mundi* (the centre of the world); it represents the Unmanifested Potential of all creation.

Yantra meditation is practised with your eyes half-open, looking at the picture of the geometric design that represents the chakra.

Working with Sound: Mantras

The power of sound is tremendous; it can inspire you by generating ideas, emotions and experiences. By merely hearing sounds your mind can undergo a variety of experiences, including both pain and pleasure. If someone shouts, "Thief! Thief!" you might jump with fright. When such is the power of an ordinary word, imagine the power potential in the subtle vibrations of mantras.

The word "mantra" comes from two Sanskrit roots: "man" meaning mind and "tra" meaning "to take across", to free, to change form or to change location. This is the root of the English words transfer, transcend, transcribe, translate, transport, travel and many others.

A mantra is a sound, a word or group of words, whose purpose is to transport your mind to a new, more positive, state of concentration. A mantra is a mystical energy encased in a sound structure. With concentration and repetition, the mantra's energy is elicited and takes form.

Most people seem to be able to concentrate on a sound more easily than a visual image or any other kind of mental form. For example, if you think about it, you can probably (mentally) hear the Beatles singing "Yellow Submarine" very clearly, even if you last heard the song many years ago. However, it is not as easy to picture clearly someone's face, even if he or she is someone you know well and saw very recently.

When mantras are reinforced and propelled by repetition, they pass from the verbal level that you are able to hear with your physical ears, through the mental and telepathic states, and on to pure thought energy. Mantra repetition is viewed as the most direct way to approach the transcendental state.

Mantras cannot be concocted or tailor-made, despite some current claims. They have always existed in a latent state as energies.

Just as gravity was discovered but not invented by Newton, mantras were revealed to the ancient masters. They were codified in the scriptures and have been handed down from teacher to student for centuries.

When it is translated, a mantra ceases to be a mantra because the sound vibrations created by the translation are different. The rhythmical vibrations of the syllables, when properly recited, help to regulate the often unsteady vibrations of your mind.

Repetition of a mantra helps to cleanse your mind of anger, greed, lust and other impurities that hide the light within.

Each chakra has associated mantras. When you work with them, make sure that you pronounce each one correctly and distinctly, neither too fast nor too slowly. Purity, concentration and a positive mental attitude all contribute greatly to the success of your practice. Repeat the mantras silently, as this is more powerful.

Chanting mantras involves focus on correct pronunciation.

Vocalization exercise: Chanting OM

Practise this exercise to prepare for working with the various sounds of the chakras. OM actually consists of three letters: A, U and M. Begin by taking a deep breath and opening your mouth as wide as possible. As you exhale, make sure that the sound begins in the pit of your abdomen and moves up through your chest and throat into your head.

- Begin with your mouth wide open and chant the sound "aah". Feel it vibrating in your abdominal area.

- As the sound moves up, round your mouth to chant "ou". Feel it vibrating in your chest and then your throat.

- Finally, allow your mouth to close as you vocalize an elongated "mmm". Feel the sound vibrating in your head and face, especially in the sinus cavities.

Continue chanting this elongated form of OM. Gradually make it softer and softer, until you are whispering it – and finally repeating it mentally. OM represents transcendental, soundless sound.

	A	U	M
Represents	Past	Present	Future
	Waking state	Dream state	Deep sleep
	Physical plane	Astral/ mental plane	Beyond mind/ intellect
Sound made with	Mouth wide open	Mouth/lips rounding	Lips shut
Sound vibrates in	Abdomen	Chest	Head and sinuses

A stone "OM" as it is written in Sanskrit.

Aids to Reflection

Keeping a journal

Merely recording facts and events does not in itself stimulate deep changes in your life. For significant transformations to take place in your core personality, keeping a journal enables you to process not only the events in your life, but also your thoughts about them. It is a powerful tool for accessing both your conscious and subconscious minds.

Your journal is a written record of your own personal reactions to questions that you pose to yourself. It is a way of connecting the teachings with your daily life and thoughts on a deeper level.

The process of writing helps you to make your feelings and experiences more tangible so that they are available to you for further development. Journal-writing stimulates movement within your subconscious mind and facilitates the surfacing of previously hidden thoughts and connections.

To keep a journal, you do not have to enjoy writing, nor do you need to be a good writer. You don't have to write full sentences, and spelling and grammar don't count; no one is going to read what you've written, except you. You are not writing your life story but rather observing the process of your own inner unfolding, working with the unique set of experiences and emotions that embody your own being. Frequently ask yourself: "What else might I do with this material"?

Write fast and don't stop. Accept whatever comes into your mind and note it down in your journal. Include your feelings, reflections, thoughts, images and whatever else comes to mind. Have a dialogue with yourself, as though you were carrying on a conversation regarding your questions. You may not reach a conclusion and you may find yourself frequently returning to re-evaluate certain points.

Your journal can be a powerful key that helps you to develop your inner life. Work with it on a regular basis and you will find that your understanding of the teachings of yoga is enhanced – and your life is greatly enriched.

Each of the chakra chapters lists some journaling questions that can help you in working with that chakra. I would suggest that it would be better to use a simple notebook rather than a beautiful one. You will feel freer to note everything that comes to your mind, without bothering to ask yourself, "Is this good enough to write down?" The best time to write is either first thing in the morning or just after your meditation practice, but you may choose to write any time when you can sit quietly and reflect on your thoughts.

Keeping a daily journal of your reflections can prove to be a great asset to your chakra work.

Practice diary

As well as a journal, keep a diary of your chakra work to ensure that you are putting your thoughts into practice. Use the thoughts that are coming up in your journal to stimulate questions for your diary (see opposite).

Keeping a practice diary helps you to establish your routine. Your diary really needs to be kept daily – preferably as the last thing you do before you go to bed at night – and it should take you no more than three to five minutes to complete. It defeats the purpose if you don't make the notations on a daily basis. If you let several days go by, you may not clearly remember what you need to write down.

Whereas your journal is about evaluation, your practice diary is a simple noting of how many exercises you performed and for how long. By making a note of quantity rather than quality, you are ensuring that you really are practising on a regular basis.

Begin by writing your "practice intention" for the week. For example, state the practice you intend to do in the coming week: "This week I will [make a positive statement] sit to meditate for 30 minutes [make an exact commitment to yourself] every morning from 7 to 7.30am [also say when/what time you will practise]. This week I will work with the _____ chakra.

This is only an example of how to write your practice intention – the details are up to you. Also, you may add your own questions relating to things you are working on, such as, "How many times did I experience anger today?". This will enable you to see the number of times decreasing steadily as you practise.

Keeping a practice diary on a regular basis helps you to overcome the tricky nature of your mind. Your mind can convince you that you have been doing a lot of practice, when in fact you haven't been doing much at all. If you make nightly entries in your diary, you will have a more accurate picture of how much practice you are actually doing.

Sample diary of weekly practice

SAMPLE QUESTIONS	MON	TUE	WED	THU	FRI	SAT	SUN	TOTAL
1. How long in chakra-balancing exercise?								
2. How long in breathing exercises?								
3. How long in meditating on chakra?								
4. How long in voluntary silence?								
5. How healthy was my diet? (Rate 1–10)								
6. How long in yoga postures?								
7. How often did I fail to be truthful?								
8. How often was I angry?								
9.								
10.								

The best times to sit for meditation are sunrise and sunset. If these times are difficult for you, try to practise first thing in the morning or last thing at night.

Perceiving your weaknesses and strengths

This meditation will help you to experience your chakras.

① Sit in a comfortable meditation position, preferably cross-legged.

② Close your eyes, seal your lips and breathe gently through your nostrils. Gradually, begin to make your breath longer.

③ Consciously direct your breath toward your solar plexus region. Observe how the energy in your belly seems to become stronger. Continue to elongate your breath until it reaches your body's base.

④ As you inhale send your breath downward along the front of your body. As you exhale, direct the energy from the base of your spine upward toward the crown of your head.

⑤ It may help you to visualize your breath as a stream of bright white light, moving from your base, all the way up to the top of your head and then down again.

⑥ As your breath flows through your body, notice whether you are able to experience the various energetic points (chakras) at:

• the base of your body

• your sacral region

• your solar plexus

• your heart

• your throat

• between your eyebrows

• the crown of your head.

⑦ Gradually move your awareness along the various energy centres in your body. Notice which one(s) you experience most strongly. Note which points are stronger and more easily experienced in front and which ones seem more dominant along the back of your body.

⑧ After a while, allow your concentration to remain on the chakra with which you are working.

⑨ At the end of each meditation, do a simple visualization exercise to ensure that you don't leave yourself too vulnerable or overly open to negative influences. Visualize each chakra in turn as a flower that is closing its petals, as flowers do in the evening.

Drawing your Chakras

You probably enjoy doing the things you do well and tend to shy away from those that you find more difficult. However, to balance your personality and your life, it is important to overcome your weaknesses. To find out where these areas are, from your own direct experience, begin by practising the meditation to help you experience your chakras on pages 68–9.

When you have finished, remain in your meditation area to draw the way your chakras feel today – not how you would like them to be. The size of the circle indicates your assessment of the relative energy of the chakra. The level of opaqueness indicates how open it is.

HOW YOUR CHAKRAS FEEL

●   Energy of the chakra is closed or blocked

○   Energy of the chakra is weak or deficient

✦   Energy of the chakra is excessive or erratic

◯   Energy of the chakra is healthy and flowing smoothly

After you have practised observing your own chakras in this way, you may find it helpful to draw your energetic relationships with others. Draw your own chakra, then the other person's corresponding chakra – use arrows to indicate the flow of energy.

SAMPLE DRAWINGS OF ENERGETIC RELATIONSHIPS

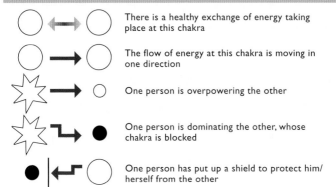

There is a healthy exchange of energy taking place at this chakra

The flow of energy at this chakra is moving in one direction

One person is overpowering the other

One person is dominating the other, whose chakra is blocked

One person has put up a shield to protect him/herself from the other

SAMPLE DRAWINGS OF ALL SEVEN CHAKRAS

Each person has a healthy sahasrara, but there is no communication taking place there

One person is slightly more open at the ajna chakra, but there is a good exchange of ideas taking place

Vishuddha chakra – mutual energy exchange

Anahata chakra – one-way flow of energy

Manipura chakra – one person dominating the other

Swadhisthana chakra – one-way flow of energy

Muladhara chakra – no energy exchange (both people are fairly ungrounded)

Meditations to Prepare for Chakra Work

Meditation is an experience unlike any other; it enables you to experience complete peace. When you meditate on your chakras, you go beyond the ordinary limits imposed by time and space. Chakra meditations are simple, yet powerful techniques for helping you to develop inner poise and keep your life in balance. These meditations are most helpful when your reinforce them with regular asana practice, self analysis and positive activities throughout the day.

Expansiveness meditation on experiencing your prana

If you work with this exercise regularly, you may begin to notice that your awareness and "boundaries" are expanding and that you are doing things that you had previously perceived to be too difficult.

❶ Sit in a comfortable meditative position with your back straight. Close your eyes and take four or five deep breaths. Then stop trying to control your breath; allow it to flow naturally through both nostrils. Let your breath be as deep or as long as it wants to be, and as fast or as slow as seems comfortable.

❷ Become aware of the parts of your body that are in contact with the floor. Consciously breathe in their direction and observe what happens. You may feel yourself expanding downward or becoming heavy. Conversely, your perception may be that you are becoming light, or you may even feel that you are floating.

❸ After a few minutes, shift your awareness to the left side of your body. Feel your energy radiating toward your left. Breathe into your left leg, side, arm, neck, cheek and temple. Send your breath to these areas. Notice how you seem to be expanding to the left.

④ Next, repeat this with the right side of your body. Feel the energy radiating toward your right. Breathe into your right leg, side, arm, neck, cheek and temple. Send your breath to these parts. See yourself expanding to the right.

⑤ Move your awareness to the rear of your body. This includes not only your back, but also the nape of your neck and back of your arms and head. Send your breath into these areas. Feel how you seem to expand outward and back.

⑥ Then come to the front of your body; feel how far your energy radiates toward your front. Move your awareness from your belly to your chest, arms, throat and face. Then feel all the parts of the front of your body simultaneously. Send your breath into these parts. Notice how you seem to expand forward.

⑦ Feel the top of your body; notice how far your energy radiates upward from each part in turn: your shoulders, head and scalp. Then feel all the top parts of your body simultaneously. Send your breath into these parts. Feel how you seem to expand upward.

⑧ Feel the expansion of your entire body. With each breath, feel yourself expanding outward in all directions. You may, if you like, repeat an affirmation, such as, "I am one with the universe" or "Nothing can stop me".

A grounded position enhances your sense of peace during meditation.

Meditation on the various layers of your being

If you are like most people who are interested in chakra work, you probably realize that there are many dimensions to life that lie beyond the apparent "reality" of your physical body. This meditation helps you to connect with the various layers of your being: physical, pranic, emotional, intellectual and karmic.

① Sit in a comfortable meditation position with your back straight. Close your eyes and breathe gently through your nostrils. Take a few deep breaths. Then stop trying to control your breath; allow it to flow naturally. Let your breath be as deep or as long as it wants to be. Permit your breath to be as fast or as slow as seems comfortable.

② Become aware of your body. To increase your awareness, bring your focus to the various parts of your body. Start by being aware of your feet, then your calves, knees, thighs, pelvis, belly, waist, chest, shoulders, arms, hands, neck and your head. This is your physical body.

③ Next, become aware that there is a deeper movement *within* this physical body; for example, the movement of your breath. If you bring your awareness one level deeper, you experience your energetic sheath – sometimes referred to as your "etheric double". This layer is more subtle than your physical body and contains the energy flow:

the prana, and also the nadis and the chakras. Spend some time observing your breath; notice its qualities as you inhale and exhale.

4 As you continue this breath-observation, you might become aware of an even more subtle movement. These are the movements of your thoughts and feelings. If you go one level deeper within your consciousness, you experience your mental–emotional sheath, containing your reactive mind, emotions and moods.

5 Observe your thoughts and feelings. Don't try to change them, just observe them; be a "silent witness". Notice what you are thinking right now. Notice how you are feeling at this moment. Be aware of your mental–emotional sheath.

6 After a while, you might realize that all your thoughts and feelings stem from a deeper source. All thoughts and feelings revolve around the experience of "I-ness". Your experience of being separate from others stems from your ego-ic sheath. This is the realm of your being where you debate with yourself and make decisions.

7 But your decision-making sheath also has a source. It arises from the most subtle layer of your being. Notice how joyful it is to experience your centre. Allow yourself to be filled with joy. Your karma is stored in this layer.

8 Finally, abandon even this layer and connect with your true "Self". This is beyond all the various layers of your being; it is an essence that is eternal and infinite.

9 After some time, gradually move your awareness outward, layer by layer. As you do, try to maintain the joyful feeling. Observe if anything has changed in your self-witnessing, in comparison to how you felt before.

CHAPTER FOUR

The Muladhara Chakra

"The goddess Kundalini dwells within
the Muladhara chakra;
She may be roused by pranayama."

Siva Samhita, 4.26

Muladhara Chakra

The muladhara chakra provides the energetic foundation of your body and mind. As your "root" chakra, it supplies you with the crucial energy of survival. This was the only focus of your life from the time you were in the womb until you were around one year old. During that stage of your development you required warmth, nourishment, stability and security; you needed to be safe and fed, but desired little else. For the most part, you were unaware of the outside world.

This chakra is the seat of your instincts. It grounds you and gives you the energy to endure life's trials and tribulations. The fight or flight response is a manifestation of the energy of muladhara.

Healing functions

Located at the base of your body, the muladhara chakra governs your auto-immune and skeletal systems, as well as your bowels and teeth. When its energy is out of balance, you may find that you suffer from frequent problems with your legs, feet, knees, base of spine, buttocks and sciatica.

MULADHARA BENEFITS

- Connecting with your body

- Insights into your relationships

- Freeing yourself from prejudices and intolerances

- Releasing yourself from inherited negative views

- Valuing all life

- Grounding yourself

- Feeling more secure in life

- Making commitments (and keeping them)

LOCATION

Base of the body

KEYWORDS

Earth, base, foundation, roots, solid, square, cube, four points of compass, security, support, wealth, stability, family, tradition, mother, nurture, nourishment, protection, grounded, gravity, smell, trust, firm

ASPIRATIONS

To connect with the earth, feel comfortable in your own body, put down roots, find the right livelihood

WORKING WITH MULADHARA

Helps your ability to overcome feelings of insecurity and release your fears

ENHANCES

Stability, commitment and grounding

Ganesha, the elephant-headed god who removes all obstacles.

Using Muladhara Chakra

Working with the energy of your muladhara chakra can assist you in connecting with your body in a healthier manner. It enhances your ability to eliminate what you no longer need or want in your life, including negative thoughts and emotions. It can help you to free yourself from prejudices and intolerances that you may have held for a long time, or even enable you to release yourself from negative ways of looking at the world that you may have "inherited" from your family.

When the muladhara energy is healthy and working well with the energy of the other chakras, you tend to value all life. You are not selfish, greedy or fearful. You look after yourself, your family and your own "group", but not at the expense of others.

Eating healthy foods, especially root vegetables, nourishes and strengthens muladhara energy.

When to work with muladhara energy

Consider working with the energy of your muladhara chakra in the following circumstances:

• You feel spaced out or disconnected from the world around you.

• You feel insecure, but can't seem to understand why.

• You feel frightened, but don't know what you are frightened of.

• You have recently, or at some time in the past, experienced a traumatic situation that you were unable to deal with on an emotional level.

• You are experiencing financial or work-related difficulties.

• You feel "stuck" in one or more aspects of your life.

• You are experiencing paralysis – either physical or psychological.

MULADHARA JOURNALING – SUGGESTED QUESTIONS

• Why am I here at this point in my life right now? You may want to begin by writing down your earliest memories. Are they happy ones?

• What belief patterns/superstitions have I inherited from my family?

• Do I perceive the world as a dangerous place?

• Do I nurture myself properly – both with food and with healthy ideas and impressions?

• Do I often feel as though I don't "belong"?

• How could I better connect with my body?

• Am I able to maintain healthy relationships? Do I let go of ones that have proved to have a negative influence on me?

• What can I do to make my eating habits less erratic? Do they reflect a lack of balanced earth energy?

• If you are raising and/or instructing children/grandchildren/students, ask yourself what qualities you would like them to inherit from you.

Symbolic Element and Energy

As you work with the energy of the muladhara chakra you will probably find yourself beginning to let go of the illusion that you can find lasting happiness in anything outside of yourself. You start to realize that true happiness lies within your own being. This important lesson has traditionally been expressed through various symbols associated with this chakra.

Meaning of name: mula = root, base, foundation; adhara = support, basis, receptacle

Position: lowest chakra, at the base of the body

Pattern of radiant energy: four-petal lotus

Element: earth = solid matter, the densest of all elements

Geometric form representing earth: metallic-yellow square, symbolizing the four corners of the earth

Symbolism of element: firmness, stability, groundedness, inertia, gravity, safety, security

Mantra (seed sound) of element: LAM

Goals: survival, safety, right livelihood, self-preservation

Age of development: womb to one year old

Consciousness: unaware of outside world; being rooted in the present moment

Female energy: Dakini (not to be confused with the Buddhist Dakinis). She has four arms, with each hand holding a weapon. In her lower right hand is a sword with which she removes fear and destroys ignorance. With the shield in her upper right hand, she offers you protection. The skull in her lower left hand encourages you not to fear death, the psychological block of the muladhara chakra. In her upper left hand she holds a trident, indicating that she represents the essence of all spiritual trinities.

Masculine custodian: Ganesha, guardian of the threshold and remover of obstacles. Without his blessings, you cannot enter this first door.

Animal: black elephant with its trunk upraised, symbolizing strength, fundamental needs for survival and the ability to ground yourself

Positive emotions: security, loyalty, sense of community

Negative emotions: Fear, prejudice, blind faith

Predominant sense: smell

Basic activity: elimination

Aspect of the life force that has its headquarters in the muladhara chakra: apana – the energy that enables you to let go of what you no longer need or want.

The Siva lingam in the muladhara chakra represents the formless Absolute. Around it, a snake is coiled three and a half times, representing your connection with the untapped infinite energy potential that is known as kundalini.

Working with the muladhara chakra can help you to gain new insights into relationships with your family members and community.

Meditating on Muladhara Yantra

1 Place the muladhara yantra on your altar (a small, low table) so that it is level to or slightly below your eyes when you are sitting for meditation.

2 Sit in your preferred position for meditation with your eyes closed. Your spine should be erect, your shoulders relaxed and your chin parallel to the ground.

3 Take a few long, slow, deep breaths, with full awareness.

4 When your body and breath are comfortable and ready, open your eyes halfway and fix your gaze on the top of the picture. Slowly rotate your eyes clockwise around its circumference.

5 Notice the four vermillion/blood-red petals. On each of these petals is a Sanskrit letter. Starting with the upper right petal, repeat the mantra as you look at it: VAM, S'AM, SHAM, SAM. Do this much only for several days, until you feel you have fully connected with the energy of these peripheral mantras.

6 When you feel ready to advance to the next level, let your eyes spiral inward as you bring your awareness to the black elephant with his upraised trunk, carrying a yellow square on his back. Both elephant and square symbolize earth, the elemental energy of the muladhara chakra.

7 The yellow square contains the seed sound of the element earth: LAM. Mentally repeat the mantra. The square also contains a Siva lingam with a serpent coiled three and a half times around it, representing the kundalini energy that lies dormant in the muladhara chakra.

Muladhara Imbalances

When the energy at your muladhara chakra is balanced and flowing freely, you feel safe and secure in your life. You tend to be fully present in the moment and connected to what is going on around you. You relate in healthy ways to the people who share your life. You are blessed with good health because your immune system is functioning properly and your skeletal system supports you. Your earthly needs, such as food and shelter, always seem to be provided.

The muladhara chakra is related to your sense of being part of a relationship, family and community. Its energy enables you to provide for your own needs and for those who may be dependent on you.

What to look for

Fear, panic, greed, sloth, intolerance, prejudice, rigidity (both mental and physical) and tendency toward blind faith are all expressions of imbalances or blockages at the muladhara chakra.

Working to balance the energy of your muladhara chakra assists you in establishing and maintaining healthy relationships with family, friends, community and work colleagues. You experience a heightened sense of security, loyalty and being a valuable member of society.

Possible causes of imbalances

A variety of traumas may cause imbalances of muladhara energy. Often they take place when you are young and usually they are beyond your control. Perhaps your birth was a painful ordeal or you were separated from your mother too early. This may have led to your having difficulty accepting nourishment.

You may have suffered extreme physical abuse, such as frequent beatings or malnourishment as child. An energetic blockage at the muladhara chakra can be caused by anything that instills panic, fright or extreme worry, including being homeless, losing your job or the divorce of your parents when you were too young to understand.

Life-threatening situations, such as those faced by holocaust survivors, war veterans, kidnap victims or people living in extreme poverty, obstruct the flow of energy. A major illness or surgery may have the same effect.

WHEN MULADHARA ENERGY IS EXCESSIVE

- You might feel stuck in life.
- You tend to be sluggish, heavy, overbearing, overburdened, overweight.
- You hoard things, have a miserly nature.
- Your thinking is in terms of black and white; you see others as being either with you or against you.
- You may suffer from constipation.
- You frequently feel depressed.
- You are obsessed with physical security.
- You are preoccupied with routine and fear change.
- You might suffer from obsessive-compulsive disorder.

WHEN MULADHARA ENERGY IS DEFICIENT

- You tend to be a fearful person.
- You lack discipline, suffer from restlessness, crave constant change.
- You may be underweight, spaced-out and ungrounded.
- You find it difficult to hold down a job.
- You are often unable to settle down, make commitments or sustain healthy relationships.
- You feel disconnected from your body.
- You live in a fantasy world and frequently resort to escapist activities.

Balancing Muladhara Energy

Being grounded and balanced are both important in life. Whatever you do, try to do it with the utmost grace and poise. Balance requires inner strength and equanimity. Being balanced may bring up other questions, such as: "How do I ground myself without getting stuck?" and "How can I build a firm foundation without my life being set in stone?"

Most people find that they are stronger and tighter in some parts of their bodies, and more relaxed and weaker in others. Balance is based on equality and requires that you strengthen your weaknesses while releasing tensions.

Standing on the earth with full awareness

You can practise this exercise daily, even while standing in a queue or waiting for a train. It enables your mind and body to reconnect with the energy of the muladhara chakra.

1 Stand up tall with your feet parallel to each other and hip-width apart. Your heels will be directly beneath your hips. Close your eyes and slowly shift your weight between your two feet, until you are satisfied that you have an equal amount of weight on each foot.

2 Notice whether your tendency is to stand back on your heels or more on your toes. Gently rock forward and back until you can feel that your centre of balance is directly over the mid-point of your arches.

3 Next, shift your weight onto the inner edges of each foot, then the outer. Make sure that all parts of your feet are supporting equal amounts of weight. Feel the ball of each toe and make sure that all 10 of them are firmly pushing into the ground.

④ Experience your shin bones pushing down into the ground. Keep your knees straight, but not locked. Feel your thigh bones pushing back, as your tailbone moves forward. Keep the lower ribs tucked under.

⑤ Bring your shoulder blades together slightly, so that your breastbone floats upward slightly. Keep your head erect with your chin parallel to the ground, and allow your breath to be rhythmic. Stand as tall as possible, as though an invisible string is pulling your body skyward. Experience how, when your body is firmly rooted, your mind feels freer.

⑥ Now that your physical posture is grounded, begin to draw parallels between this and the various issues in your life. Ask yourself the question: "Where do I stand in life?"

If your posture is balanced, a line drawn downward from the centre of your skull would pass through your shoulder, slightly behind your hip joint, slightly in front of your knee joint and through the arches of your feet.

Axis of balance

Muladhara Relationships

Your root chakra may be compared to an antenna that constantly sends and receives energetic information relating to your physical survival and sense of security. You began this type of communication with others long before you were able to think in words or concepts.

When you relate to other people, the muladhara interactions tend to be concerned with wealth, nourishment and grounding. For example, the partners of a successful business would probably (unconsciously) connect through their root chakras when discussing finances. But they would do well, when discussing their "vision" for the company, to also involve the ajna or third eye chakra in their communication.

The connection between a parent and child is instinctive and relates to the energy of the muladhara chakra.

When you are walking down a dark street late at night and feel afraid, it may be that your muladhara antenna is picking up danger signals from the environment. When this happens, it is often helpful to take a few deep grounding breaths that will provide you with a foundation of strength.

Instinctive connections

As a young child your energetic connection with your mother was primarily via your muladhara chakra. This was the main means by which you received instinctive, survival information. Yet it is likely that your mother's connection to you was not only a nurturing one via the root chakra, but also involved her feelings of love through her heart chakra.

Many of your basic perceptions of the world and your relative place in society were probably not learned verbally, but were received as energetic information via your muladhara chakra. To get a better understanding of this instinctive communication, try finishing the following sentence quickly, without thinking for too long: "Everyone in my family/community/who lives in my house is …".

If you are a parent, grandparent or caregiver, one way to enhance your energetic relationship through the muladhara chakra is to visualize a stream of golden light flowing from the base of your spine to that of your child, grandchild or patient. This light can be particularly nurturing in times of danger and in stressful situations.

A NURTURING AND LOVING ENERGETIC CONNECTION

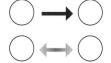

mother   child

Mother's love received through anahata (heart) chakra

Nurturing energetic connection at muladhara (root) chakra

Muladhara Meditations

Meditation on your muladhara chakra frees you from the idea that you can obtain lasting happiness from anything in a solid state. It enables you to master the cravings of your sense of smell. You gain the ability to eliminate what you no longer need in your body – and what you no longer want in your life. You become able to let go of negative thoughts and emotions. Your body and mind lose all sluggishness, yet you are not ungrounded.

Affirmations

Kneel with your knees and feet together. If you prefer, you may sit in a simple cross-legged position or even in a chair with your feet flat on the ground. Be aware of the pull of gravity and its effects on your body. Rest the backs of your hands on your thighs in the earth mudra: join the tips of your ring finger and thumb on each hand, keeping the remaining fingers relaxed. Mentally repeat one of the following affirmations:

• I am exactly where I need to be.

• I am nurtured by the energy of the earth.

• My body supports me with its strength.

If you feel the need to sit on a chair for meditation, make sure that your feet are flat on the floor and grounded.

Walking meditation

Feeling the ground under your feet, you begin to understand the earth, the element of the muladhara chakra. This walking meditation may be practised alone or with any number of people. You may choose to walk in a straight line or in a circle. Be totally aware of each step. If others are involved, maintain a measured distance of an arm's length between yourself and the person in front of you.

Walking meditation is best done barefoot on the earth herself, but it may also be practised indoors. Watch your entire body being involved in the action. See how each knee bends, lifts and then straightens. Be aware of the movement of your ankles, hips, spine and shoulders. Keep bringing your attention back to the soles of your feet and their interaction with the earth.

① With your eyes half-open, fix your gaze at the ground approximately 2ft (60cm) in front of your feet. Hold your left hand on top of your right hand at waist level with the palms upward.

② Begin to walk rhythmically taking slow, short steps. Pay total attention to your movement.

③ Tune each step to your breath. Inhale as you very slowly lift your foot. Move your foot forward no more than 3–4in (8–10cm) and exhale as you lower it to the ground. As each foot touches the ground, feel it rooting itself deeply.

To make the earth mudra, join the tip of your ring finger to the tip of your thumb; relax the other fingers. This mudra enhances your body's stability and helps to remove physical weakness.

Working with Muladhara

The root chakra grounds your physical existence. It connects your body with the earth's energy system. Proper and unrestricted energy flow through the muladhara chakra is necessary for healthy growth. If you lack connection with the earth, your physical health and well-being will tend to deteriorate.

Vajrasana – Thunderbolt pose

① Kneel on the ground so that you are sitting with your buttocks resting firmly on your heels.

② Keep your feet together; you may prefer to have your knees together or slightly apart. Rest your hands lightly on your thighs. Feel as though you are rooting yourself firmly, drawing stability and strength from the ground. Pay particular attention to the pull of gravity and its effects on your body. With practice, you will experience a pleasant heaviness that becomes a feeling of stability and stillness. Sit for as long as you feel comfortable.

Balasana – Child's pose

① Begin by sitting on your heels in vajrasana.

② Bend forward until your forehead is on the ground. If there is any tension in your body when attempting this, place a cushion or block in front of your knees and allow your forehead to rest on it. Rest your hands, palms upward, on the ground on either side of your feet. Feel as though you are sinking down into the pose. Remain in the pose for as long as you feel comfortable.

Ardho-mukhshwanasana – Downward-facing dog

① Begin on your hands and knees. Tuck your toes under and slowly straighten your knees.

Vajrasana –
Thunderbolt pose

Balasana –
Child's pose

Ardho-mukhshwanasana –
Downward-facing dog

Padagushtasana –
Standing forward bend

Trikonasana –
Triangle pose

② Lift your hips and bring your chest as close to your thighs as possible. Hold for at least 30 seconds, increasing to 3 minutes.

Padagushtasana – Standing forward bend

① Stand erect with your feet slightly apart. Inhale as you lift your arms up next to your ears, keeping your elbows straight.

② Exhale as you bend forward and down as far as possible. Keep your knees straight and hold your ankles or the backs of your shins or knees. Breathe as you remain in the position, with your weight on the balls of your feet. Lift your hips as high as possible. Hold for 10 seconds, gradually increasing to 1 minute.

Trikonasana – Triangle pose

① Step your feet wide apart – wider than your shoulders. Bring your arms straight out to your sides at shoulder level, parallel to the ground with your palms facing downward.

② Turn your left foot out at a 90-degree angle and rotate your right foot inward to a 45-degree angle. Keeping your arms in line with your shoulders, lengthen your rib cage to your left. Reach down with your left hand and rest it on your left leg. If you can't reach your ankle, hold your shin or thigh. Breathe deeply and hold the pose for 10 seconds, gradually increasing to 30 seconds.

③ Release the pose and repeat the triangle on the other side.

Utkatasana – Chair pose

① (See picture on page 99.) Stand with your feet 5–6in (15cm) apart and parallel to each other. Look at a point straight in front of you. Bring your arms straight out in front of you at shoulder level, parallel to the floor with your palms facing downward.

② Keeping your heels on the ground as much as possible, bend your knees as though you are about to sit on a chair. Focus on your breath as you hold the position for at least 10 seconds.

③ Lean back a little and try to sit down a bit more. Keep your chest up as much as possible and tuck your tailbone in. Hold the pose for 10–30 seconds.

④ Come out of the pose and relax for a moment. Repeat the pose two to five times.

Viradhadrasana – Warrior pose

① Stand with your feet wide apart and bring your arms straight out from your shoulders. Turn your left foot out and your right foot slightly inward. Slowly bend your left knee, keeping it in line with your foot. Look at your left hand, trying not to lean toward it.

② Bring your body back to the centre and repeat the pose on the other side. Try to hold for 10 seconds on each side, gradually increasing to 1 minute.

Vrikshasana – Tree pose

① Stand erect with your feet slightly apart; bend your right knee and place your right foot flat on the inside of your left thigh. Bring your palms together at your chest, saluting the earth.

② Then straighten your elbows and extend your arms upward, with your fingers pointing toward the sky.

Other movements for muladhara

Squats, walking in squats, "elephant walk" (stepping heavily with your body bent over and your arms swinging to mimic an elephant's trunk), easy marching

Viradhadrasana –
Warrior pose

Vrikshasana –
Tree pose

Utkatasana –
Chair pose

CHAPTER FIVE

The Swadhisthana Chakra

"Meditation on the pure lotus, which is named
Swadhisthana, frees you from the control
of your enemies, such as egoism, ignorance,
lust and greed."

Sat-Cakra-Nirupana, verse 18

Swadhisthana Chakra

The swadhisthana chakra is associated with your creative instincts and pleasure impulse. When its energy is balanced and unblocked, you experience fluidity and grace in your life and are able to accept and adapt to change. The sacral chakra is the seat of your instinct of procreation. It is not necessarily concerned with your personal survival, but rather with your gratification. Its power lies in self-fulfilment, as opposed to the self-centred energy of muladhara.

Symbolized by the water element, the swadhisthana energy is what enables you to move and change. It is about balance in your life, and the ability to engage in a healthy give and take with others.

If you are able to maintain an equilibrium of swadhisthana energy, you will tend to feel more comfortable with yourself. You will be able to give your energy to others, but also to recognize that your own needs in life are important, too.

Healing functions

Located in the middle region of your lower back, the swadhisthana chakra governs the liquid elements of your body – blood, lymph, tears, urine and saliva. It is responsible for maintaining your body's liquid levels, as well as the viscosity of your blood. When the energy of the sacral chakra is out of balance, you may suffer from problems with your kidneys, urinary tract or reproductive system. You may have trouble physically expressing your emotions.

SWADHISTHANA BENEFITS

- Increasing your vitality, sensitivity and creative abilities

- Expressing your emotions in healthier ways

- Feeling more confident and able to express yourself

LOCATION

Sacral region; middle of the lower back

KEYWORDS

Water, wet, fluid, flexible, flow, changeable, unpredictable, unstable, dreams, pleasure, fun, contentment, guilt, "crocodile tears", letting go, lotus, instinct, taste. Associations often experienced in terms of taste: "savour the feeling".

ASPIRATIONS

To connect with life's flow, be happy, be comfortable with yourself, believe that you are entitled to happiness and pleasure in your life

WORKING WITH SWADHISTHANA

Augments your ability to overcome feelings of guilt, shame and unworthiness

ENHANCES

Flow and flexibility

Water and its fluidity of movement best describe the energy of the swadhisthana chakra.

Using Swadhisthana Chakra

Working with the energy of your swadhisthana chakra can assist you in increasing your vitality, sensitivity and creative abilities. It may also make you seem more physically and sexually attractive.

Balancing swadhisthana energy can enhance your ability to express your emotions in healthier ways. If you tend toward addictive behaviour, it may even inspire you to enter a 12-step programme, or, if you are already in a programme, to enhance your involvement.

When the energy of your swadhisthana chakra is unblocked and vibrating at a healthy level, you feel more confident and better able to express yourself without fear of rejection. You don't need to resort to emotional manipulation to get your way. You probably convey the energy of swadhisthana chakra in your daily life when you use expressions associated with taste, such as "sweet dreams", "bitter experiences" or "a relationship going sour".

Varuna, god of the waters, is associated with the fluid energy of the swadhisthana chakra. He is often pictured riding on the mythological animal known as the makara.

When to work with swadhisthana energy

• You feel stuck in your life.

• You need to move on, but can't let go of negative emotions or unhealthy attachments to particular people or situations.

• It is time to release the idea of getting "closure" in relationships that will probably never be resolved.

• You would like to create more flexibility and flow in various aspects of your life.

• You crave a greater ability to "taste" what life has to offer.

• You feel sexually blocked, or ashamed of the body's functions.

• You would like to overcome your preoccupations with shame, jealousy and lust.

• You are ready to make a fearless moral inventory of yourself.

• It is time to stop using sexual and emotional manipulations. You realize that these are not healthy means of getting what you want.

SWADHISTHANA JOURNALING — SUGGESTED QUESTIONS

• Do I believe myself unworthy of being happy?

• How do I express my views about gender roles?

• Do I feel stuck in my life in general? Is my job the problem?

• Can I maintain lasting and healthy relationships with others?

• Am I able to set healthy personal boundaries?

• How can I be open to positive changes without losing inner balance?

• Am I able to enjoy life? How might I keep myself from becoming addicted to pleasure?

• Do I feel frustrated in achieving my dreams?

• How realistic are my plans for the future?

Symbolic Element and Energy

As you work with the swadhisthana energy, you will find yourself better able to let go of things, relationships and situations that you no longer need or which no longer exert a positive influence on your life. This positive, creative flow is symbolized by the various aspects of the chakra.

Meaning of name: swa = your own essential nature; swad = sweet; sthana = place, residence. The name of this chakra can be translated as "your own home" – or as the "sweet place", i.e. your pleasure centre. It is the realm of "swapna", the dream state, the abode of illusions.

Position: second from lowest chakra, in the sacral region of your lower back

Pattern of radiant energy: six-petal lotus

Element: water = liquid matter

Geometric form representing water: watery, pale-blue circle with a crescent moon inside

Symbolism of element: flowing, flexibility, fluidity, adaptive

Mantra (seed sound) of element: VAM

Goals: self-gratification, healthy sexuality, movement, pleasure, emotional balance, physical creativity, physical love

Age of development: six months–two years

Consciousness: becoming aware of others; beginning to move around the world

Female energy: Rakini, the two-headed concierge of the swadhisthana chakra holds the key to maintaining a healthy balance between stability and flow. She enables you to let go of fantasy while holding on to your dreams. Her face is beautiful and inspiring, if you follow restraint in gratifying your desires. But she appears frightful if you are a slave to your passions.

Masculine custodian: Varuna, god of water, controls the legendary nectar of immortality, as well as the life-giving substance of blood. The noose in his hand symbolizes his control of the animal nature.

Animal: makara – a mythological animal that resembles a crocodile with a fish's tail. The makara represents the essential vigour of your body – as in Chinese medicine, the kidney energy is your basic strength and stamina.

Positive emotions: sensitive, idealistic

Negative emotions: guilt, blame, lust, shame, betrayal, jealousy, envy, sexual perversions, desire for pornography, manipulation, deviousness, displaying false emotions – "shedding crocodile tears"

Predominant sense: taste

Basic activity: reproduction – the basic energy of creativity

Aspect of life force that has its headquarters in swadhisthana chakra: apana, the energy that enables you to give birth – whether to a child, a project or a work of art

Working with the swadhisthana chakra can help you to get new insight into balancing your emotions.

Meditating on Swadhisthana Yantra

① Place a picture of the chakra on your meditation table, slightly below your eye level.

② Sit in your preferred meditation position with your eyes closed. Ensure that your body is straight, but relaxed.

③ Take a few long, slow, deep breaths, with full awareness, until your breath is calm and slow. With each exhalation, feel that all negativity, tiredness, stress and impurities are leaving your body.

④ When you feel ready, open your eyes halfway. Fix your gaze on the upper right-hand corner of the yantra, at approximately "one o'clock". Begin to rotate your eyes clockwise around the circumference of the picture.

⑤ Notice the six deep-red petals with Sanskrit letters written on them. These represent qualities that meditation on the swadhisthana yantra will help you to get rid of: over-indulgence, pitilessness, self-destructiveness, delusion, disdain and suspicion.

⑥ After some time, allow your eyes to slowly spiral inward. You will notice a makara, a mythological animal that resembles a crocodile with a fish's tail. On his back, the makara carries a watery, pale-blue circle with a crescent moon at the bottom. This is the symbol of water, the element of swadhisthana – and the moon that controls the waters. Inside the circle is the Sanskrit letter "VAM", the seed mantra for Varuna, god of water.

⑦ Eventually you will find yourself at the centre of the yantra. Try to hold your concentration there, preferably on the bindu. This is the energetic centre of the yantra; it is the point over the Sanskrit letter that forms the inner seed mantra.

Swadhisthana Imbalances

When the energy of your swadhisthana chakra is balanced and flowing freely, you are able to accept change without resistance, to "go with the flow". Contrary to popular perception, working with the sacral chakra is not about enhancing your sexuality. For the swadhisthana to be fully open and balanced, your sex drive must be sublimated into a force of awareness. Opening the sacral chakra is more about letting go of guilt and frustration, and being able to enjoy the uncertainties of life.

What to look for

You suffer from guilt, jealousy and restlessness. You may be plagued with chronic lower back pain or sciatica. If you are a woman, you may have frequent gynecological problems, pelvic pain or kidney and bladder problems. Men and women with imbalances in the swadhisthana chakra often suffer from sexual problems, such as impotence or infertility. You may be overly possessive or too clinging in your relationships.

Possible causes of imbalances

Often the traumas that cause imbalance are related to sexuality: being forced into an adult sexual role too early, sexual abuse, incest, rape or abortion. Or your imbalance can be the result of having been neglected as a child or having suffered rejection, emotional abuse and/or manipulation.

Perhaps you come from a family where there is a religious or moral aversion to pleasure. You might come from a family in which there was alcoholism, or one in which physical and psychological abuse was accepted as the norm.

WHEN SWADHISTHANA ENERGY IS EXCESSIVE

- Nothing in your life seems good enough.

- Your sexuality may be confused, unless the excessive swadhisthana energy is balanced by the influence of the heart chakra.

- You may engage in frequent emotional and sexual manipulations.

- Your life is in a constant state of flux.

- You have the tendency to be overly emotional and sensitive.

- You may be addicted to sex, pornography or sexual perversions, or to pleasure or excitement in general.

- You have problems setting personal boundaries for yourself and allow others to invade your privacy.

WHEN SWADHISTHANA ENERGY IS DEFICIENT

- You are extremely introverted.

- You tend to be depressed.

- You experience excessive stiffness in your body.

- You are rigid in your attitudes, with unyielding self-imposed boundaries.

- You deny yourself even minimal pleasures and fear sex. This is very different from simple living and practising celibacy as a spiritual practice. You may be frigid or impotent.

- You dread change and are unable to see how your life could improve.

- You probably lack initiative; you need to be told what to do, rather than being a "self-starter".

- You suffer from emotional numbness, feeling that you don't deserve to be happy and that you are unable to enjoy yourself.

Balancing Swadhisthana Energy

Even when you are careful to not be too open, you may pick up some unwanted energies through the swadhisthana chakra. This may happen at work or while you are commuting, walking down the street or in some other place full of strangers. Water, the element of swadhisthana energy, helps you to counteract the negative effects of unwanted energetic toxins. An energy-cleansing bath often proves helpful.

Energy-cleansing bath

The principle of this bath is to rejuvenate the balance of your swadhisthana energy, as well as to cleanse your body. Use sea salt, Epsom salts or magnesium sulphate to draw toxins out of the body. For a refreshing effect, you can also add 5–10 drops of swadhisthana-balancing essential oils:

- **Clary sage** encourages the meditative state that Australian aborigines call Dreamtime; this is the realm of swadhisthana energy.

- **Cypress** helps you to go with the new flow when there has been a major change in your life, such as a career change or the death of someone close.

- **Frankincense** helps to wash away old energies that may block your spiritual growth when you add a few drops to a pre-meditation bath. It enhances tranquility and insight.

- **Marjoram** helps to clear out feelings of guilt, an emotion associated with the swadhisthana chakra. It also promotes celibacy, should you be so inclined.

- **Patchouli** will discourage you from becoming too dreamy during meditation; it will bring you back into your body.

THE SWADHISTHANA CHAKRA

Add approximately two cups of your chosen salts to your tub of water. Soak in the bath for 10–20 minutes. This will eliminate excess energy and toxins, and maintain a healthy body. If you prefer to take an energy-cleansing shower, you can make your own exfoliating scrub. Put 5–10 drops of your chosen oil into a cup of olive oil, then mix in a handful of salts. Rub your body with some of this mixture, then shower off immediately. This will help you to eliminate unwanted energies.

Natural salts are excellent as energy cleansers, especially when used with essential oils.

Swadhisthana Relationships

Your sacral chakra may be compared to an antenna that constantly picks up and sends out energetic information relating to your emotional equilibrium and your ability to adapt. It also transmits your capacity for physical creativity, pleasure and sexuality.

Your swadhisthana chakra connects you to others through feelings, desires and sensations. It enables you to understand non-verbal communication, not only with other people but also with animals, plants and all of nature. The swadhisthana chakra makes you aware of how the world responds to you. You experience physical attraction to or repulsion from someone through this chakra.

A healthy marriage that lasts involves an exchange of energies at both the swadhisthana and anahata chakras.

THE SWADHISTHANA CHAKRA

114

Instinctive power, or balance of power, is the basis of swadhisthana relationships. These can be negatively expressed in terms of sex, money and betrayal ("they stabbed me in the back"), rape and the need for revenge. Or, within a relationship, there may be an excess of fire.

It is important to be able to discern when to open and close your second chakra. You may want to open up emotionally when you are with friends or family members or sexually with your partner, yet you wouldn't want to have the same openness when you walk down a crowded street.

Forging a lasting relationship

Lovers may connect heart to heart, or more instinctively. A relationship may begin with him relating from the swadhisthana chakra and her relating from the anahata or heart chakra. If her heart energy is able to stimulate his heart chakra, this could develop into a very healthy long-term relationship.

A healthy long-term partnership (as in a successful marriage) needs to include a give and take of energies at both the heart and sacral chakras. This means that each person relates to the other in a loving, as well as a sexual way. Such a partnership also needs to include muladhara relationships, to help deal with finances and to give the family stability.

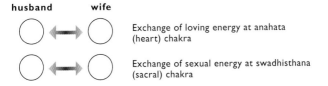

A GIVE AND TAKE OF ENERGIES

husband   **wife**

Exchange of loving energy at anahata (heart) chakra

Exchange of sexual energy at swadhisthana (sacral) chakra

Swadhisthana Meditations

Meditation on your swadhisthana chakra frees you from the idea that you can gain lasting happiness from anything that is in a liquid state. You expand your mastery over your sense of taste, and you conquer your six enemies: lust, anger, greed, pride, envy and egotism. Your body and mind become fluid, adaptable and pure.

Practise the following meditations sitting in a comfortable meditation position. Do not lie down as you will tend to fall asleep. Rest the backs of your hands on your thighs in the water mudra: join the tips of your little finger and thumb on each hand, and allow the remaining fingers to be relaxed.

Affirmations

Mentally repeat one of the following:

• With utmost grace, I adapt to my situation in life.

• I abandon myself to the flow of divine energy.

• My mind is ever-balanced.

• I rejoice when others succeed; I am free of jealousy and envy.

• I welcome healthy change into my life.

Visualizing your mind as a lake

1 Sit in a comfortable meditation position of your choice. Close your eyes. Breathe gently through both nostrils, with your lips sealed. Imagine that your mind is a lake.

2 Imagine that someone has dropped a large, beautiful diamond into the lake. Allow your breath to become progressively shallower, until it is just coming to the end of your nostrils. By doing this, your breath won't make any ripples on the surface of the lake.

◈3 As your breath becomes calmer, so will your mind. Now focus all of your attention on seeing the diamond beneath the waters.

◈4 If you notice your mind drifting off, keep bringing it back to this point of focus.

◈5 If other thoughts start to arise in your mind, do not try to drive them away. The more you try, the more they will return and gain strength. They will tax your energy. Become indifferent to other things that are happening in your mind and focus your attention solely on the diamond. The other thoughts will gradually disperse.

◈6 When the surface of a lake is still you can see to the bottom clearly. When the surface is agitated by waves, this is impossible. The same is true of your mind. When it is still you will experience profound inner peace.

Water mudra promotes the balance of the water element in your body. It helps to restores moisture to your skin and other organs.

Working with Swadhisthana

The energy of the sacral chakra enables you to feel at ease in your life. It gives fluidity to your movements, supple strength to your mind and it enables you to adapt to your environment. Yoga postures that enhance hip and pelvic flexibility help this energy flow.

Janu-sirshasana – Single-legged forward bend

① Sit on the ground with your legs straight out in front of you. Bend your left knee and place your left foot flat against the inside of your right thigh. Bring your left knee down toward the ground as far as you can without forcing it. Keep your right knee straight.

② Inhale, lifting both of your arms straight up over your head.

③ Exhale as you bend forward from your hips. Catch hold of your right foot (use a strap if necessary) and bring your breastbone toward your right thigh. Breathe deeply as you hold the pose for 10–30 seconds, then inhale as you stretch up to the starting position.

④ Repeat the pose on the other side.

Badha-konasana – Bound-angle pose

① Sit on the ground, bend your knees and bring the soles of your feet together. Bring your knees out toward the sides and allow them to drop toward the ground.

② Hold your feet together with your hands as you gently lower your chest toward your feet. Sit in this position for 10–30 seconds.

Chandrasana – Kneeling crescent moon

① Get on your hands and knees, with your knees and feet together. Place your right foot flat on the ground in front of you. Bring your palms together at your chest.

Janu-sirshasana –
Single-legged forward bend

Badha-konasana –
Bound-angle pose

Chandrasana –
Kneeling crescent
moon

② Straighten your elbows, stretching them up and back. Arch your body back, keeping your palms flat. Hold for 10–30 seconds.

③ Come back to the starting position and repeat on the other side.

Kalikasana – Goddess squat

Stand with your feet 3ft (1m) apart. Turn your toes out to a 45-degree angle. Bend your knees and squat down as much as possible, with your back straight and tailbone tucked under. Keep your knees in line with your feet. Bring your palms together at your chest, using your elbows to push your knees out. Hold for 30–60 seconds.

Matsyasana – Fish pose

① Lie flat on your back with your legs out straight. Bring your legs together. Place your hands under your thighs.

② Bend your elbows, pushing them into the ground. Arch your chest upward and place the crown of your head gently onto the floor. Hold, with your weight mainly on your elbows. Breathe as deeply as possible, imagining that your ribs are opening to pull in oxygen and prana. Hold for about 30 seconds, building to 2 minutes.

③ To come out of the position lift your head slightly and slide it back as you lower your upper body to the ground.

Sethu-bandhasana – The bridge

① Lie on your back with your knees bent and your feet flat on the floor. Your feet should be parallel and hip-width apart.

② Lift your hips as high as possible. Place your hands flat on your back with your fingers pointing in toward your spine and your thumbs up toward ceiling. Hold the pose for 10–30 seconds. Come down and relax for a moment. Repeat two to three times.

Other movements for swadhisthana

Hip openers, swimming, hula hooping, belly dancing

**Kalikasana –
Goddess squat**

**Matsyasana –
Fish pose**

**Sethu-bandhasana –
The bridge**

CHAPTER SIX

The Manipura Chakra

"In the same way that the sun continually radiates energy to the planets, manipura chakra radiates and distributes pranic energy throughout the entire human framework, regulating and energizing the activity of the various organs, systems and processes of life."

Swami Satyananda Saraswati, *Kundalini Tantra*

INTRODUCING

Manipura Chakra

Your solar plexus chakra provides the transformational power for your body and mind to be able to process matter and energy. It converts whatever you take in – whether food or ideas – into a more usable form. Manipura houses your most prized possession, which is your sense of self. It is the seat of your personality and your charisma; how well it functions determines how the world sees you.

The "element" of this chakra is fire. As the sun, fire gives life to everything on earth. Without heat in your body, you would not be alive. In Indian tradition, weddings take place in front of the fire, which acts as the witness to the vows. In a fire ceremony, the flames transform the offerings and prayers, and carry their essence to the gods. Thus, fire is the messenger and conduit between dimensions; it is the interface between the physical world and higher realms.

Healing functions

Located in your solar plexus region, the manipura chakra is the base of what is known in ayurveda as "digestive fire". Digestion is the process by which your body changes matter into usable energy and takes place when you carry out any kind of activity in which energy is used. The functioning of both your digestive system and your muscles is said to be controlled by the manipura chakra.

MANIPURA BENEFITS

• Establishing healthy boundaries

• Strengthening will-power and assertiveness

• Connecting with, and understanding, your own power

• Improving digestion and metabolism

• Boosting stamina, but also helping you know when to quit

LOCATION

Solar plexus; the region just below your rib cage and above the navel.

KEYWORDS

Fire, heat, light, transformation, assimilation, digestion, hunger, messenger, witness, pro-active, body's stronghold, fortress, power centre, will-power, personal power, empower, ambition, honour, integrity, charisma, sight, radiance, enliven, excite, arouse, courage, independence, passion

ASPIRATIONS

To invigorate your other chakras, as well as your body and mind

WORKING WITH MANIPURA

Gives you the strength to transform your life, enabling you to "turn over a new leaf"

ENHANCES

Self-esteem, self-discipline, self-reliance

In Indian tradition, fire, the element of manipura chakra, is the witness to important occasions such as marriages.

Using Manipura Chakra

Working with the energy of your manipura chakra can assist you in establishing healthy boundaries for your life. It can also enable you to strengthen your will-power and assertiveness, thus enhancing your ability to stand up for what you think is right.

Tuning into the manipura chakra enables you to connect with and understand the nature of your own personal power. It gives you the strength to command with authority, also to organize and manage your life more successfully.

On a physical level, working with the manipura chakra may improve your digestion, metabolism and assimilation of vital nutrients. Your mind and body tend to become radiant, with a healthy shine to your skin and eyes. It can increase your natural immunity, and lead to better health and a long, productive life. Balancing your manipura energy may boost your stamina, but it also enhances your ability to know when it is time to quit.

When to work with manipura energy

- You notice that you are apologizing too frequently.

- You tend to be meek, overly modest, unassuming and self-effacing.

- You are inclined to force your ideas onto others. You may be a "passive-aggressive" person, who controls others while appearing to be totally undemanding.

- You frequently procrastinate.

- You feel as though you are a victim of your circumstances.

- You need to rely on caffeine or stimulants to "get going".

- You are finding it increasingly difficult to look after your own welfare.

- You are suffering from nervous exhaustion.

Agni, the fire god, is pictured here riding on a ram, the animal that symbolizes the manipura chakra.

MANIPURA JOURNALING — SUGGESTED QUESTIONS

- What is the one thing in my life that most depletes me?
- Why do I allow other people to drain me of energy?
- How do I "see" myself?
- Do I tend to be an angry and irritable person?
- Do I have difficulty with authority figures?
- Do I sometimes feel powerless?
- Is my happiness really in the hands of others?
- How could I transform my doubts and fears into positive energy?
- What great things could I achieve if I were more enthusiastic?
- How could my food allergies/intolerances be related to my self-confidence?

Symbolic Element and Energy

Personal transformation involves taking risks. Working with manipura energy empowers you to develop the courage to face life's challenges and to not be afraid of assuming personal responsibility for the outcome. This formidable lesson is symbolized by the elements representing the manipura chakra.

Meaning of name: mani = shining jewel; pura = city

Position: third from lowest chakra, in the region of your solar plexus

Pattern of radiant energy: 10-petal lotus

Element: fire = radiant matter, heat, light

Geometric form representing fire: upward-pointing, fiery-red triangle

Symbolism of element: transformation

Mantra (seed sound) of element: RAM

Goals: self-reliance; acceptance of your unique identity; a healthy self-image

Age of development: 18 months–four years (the terrible twos)

Consciousness: relating to others as an independent individual

Female energy: Lakini shines like a precious jewel. Her body is the colour of molten gold and her blessings are necessary for your success in life – that is, you need drive and ambition to accomplish your goals.

   With each of her four hands Lakini makes a different symbolic gesture. (1) She holds the fire that represents life itself, and also purification. (2) She has one palm upraised as a blessing and a plea for you to be fearless. (3) She holds a thunderbolt, representing the energy of nature. (4) She holds an arrow, which symbolizes the impetus to hit your goal in life. With swadhisthana, your goal was sensual pleasure; at manipura you are aiming at personal freedom and self-reliance.

Masculine custodian: Agni is the god and guardian of fire. He represents the vital spark of life that is in all living beings. He never ages and is also immortal. From "agni" comes the Latin "ignis", which is the root of the English words "ignite" and "initiation".

Agni is the fire that digests your food. He is the fire of the sun and the lightning bolt. The stars are sparks from Agni's flame. He is the "fire in the belly" – that is, the impetus to get things done.

Animal: ram or billy goat – a proud and often-angry beast, who charges at life head-on

Positive emotions: drive, dedication, stamina, perseverance, firmness of resolve, pride in work well done, self-discipline

Negative emotions: anger, rage, bitterness, vanity, pride, resentment, attraction to black magic, stubbornness

Predominant sense: sight

Basic activity: transportation – movement of your muscles

Aspect of life force that has its headquarters in manipura chakra: samana – the energy that enables you to digest/process what you take in (whether it is food, air or ideas)

Working with the manipura chakra can help you to gain new insights into your self-image.

Meditating on Manipura Yantra

1 Place a picture of the manipura chakra on your meditation table, slightly below your eye level. Sit in front of it, in your preferred meditation position, with your eyes closed. Take a few long, slow, deep breaths, with full awareness.

2 When you feel ready, fix your gaze on the upper right-hand corner of the yantra, at approximately "one o'clock". Begin to rotate your eyes clockwise around the circumference of the picture.

3 Notice the 10 deep-purple petals containing Sanskrit mantras. These represent qualities that meditation on this yantra will help you to get rid of (shame, treachery, jealousy, thirst, spiritual ignorance, sadness, delusion, disgust, foolishness and fear):

- DAM DHAM NAM – pronounced with your tongue on the roof of your mouth.
- TAM THAM DAM DHAM – your tongue is touching your teeth.
- NAM PAM PHAM – you are using your lips to make the sound.

4 After some time, allow your eyes to begin to spiral inward slowly. You will notice a ram, a very angry animal who is always looking for a fight. He represents the fiery nature of the manipura chakra. On his back, the ram carries the flame-red, downward-pointing triangle that is the symbol of fire, the element of manipura.

Notice the triangle has three "feet" – these may also be understood as gateways to the essence of the yantra, or as the handles of a cooking pot. Inside the triangle is the Sanskrit letter "RAM", the seed mantra for Agni, guardian of fire.

5 You are now at the energetic centre of the yantra. Try to hold your concentration there, preferably on the bindu, the dot over the large Sanskrit letter.

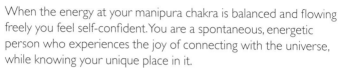

Manipura Imbalances

When the energy at your manipura chakra is balanced and flowing freely you feel self-confident. You are a spontaneous, energetic person who experiences the joy of connecting with the universe, while knowing your unique place in it.

The manipura chakra is related to your will-power, personal power and self-esteem. Its energy is what enables you to set reasonable personal boundaries, as well as maintain a healthy sense of honour and integrity.

What to look for

Anger, rage, excessive vanity, bitterness and resentment are all expressions of imbalances or blockages of energy at the manipura chakra. These negative emotions are energetically stored in your solar plexus region, often for many years. This happens whether you are irritated by small things and get angry easily, or stoically resist any external expression.

Possible causes of imbalances

Often traumas that cause blockages or imbalances of energy at the manipura chakra are related to your sense of personal power. Perhaps you had an overbearing parent or teacher – or you were a victim of bullying, scapegoating or shaming. Maybe you were forced to assume responsibilities that were inappropriate for your age. Or, at some point in your life, you may have felt that someone was trying to break your will or dehumanize you in some way. Distortions of manipura energy can be the result of anything that would have caused you to lose your self-confidence or to feel that others were controlling your life.

WHEN MANIPURA ENERGY IS EXCESSIVE

- You tend to be overly individualistic and perhaps eccentric.

- You tend to be judgmental, intolerant and lacking in sensitivity.

- You are frequently angry and irritable.

- You have difficulty with authority figures.

- You tend to be self-centred, aggressive, constantly active.

- You are prone to temper tantrums and violent outbursts.

- You feel the need to control others and like to have the last word.

- The inability to understand the nature of your own power often leads to misuse of power. You may even have a sadistic streak.

- You are over-competitive and don't know when to quit.

- You may suffer from digestive problems, such as heartburn or ulcers.

WHEN MANIPURA ENERGY IS DEFICIENT

- You have no "fire" or enthusiasm, no ambition or drive; you lack energy to put your ideas into practice.

- You tend to be weak-willed, passive and lacking in self-confidence. You may suffer from low self-esteem and poor self-image, and have difficulty in setting reasonable personal boundaries.

- You frequently feel powerless, needy and may have a victim mentality.

- You have difficulty in taking responsibility for your own health and tend to surrender your personal power to others.

- You will probably tend to procrastinate frequently.

- You lack stamina.

- You may need stimulants, such as caffeine, on a regular basis.

- You need the approval of others and worry about what "they" will think.

Balancing Manipura Energy

When your digestive fire, which has its seat in your solar plexus region, is strong and balanced, you digest your food well, absorb plentiful vital energy from the air you breathe and have an intelligent relationship with the world around you. Conversely, when there is a blockage, you have a greater tendency to suffer from chronic conditions and psychological imbalances.

Abstaining from solid food to fast on juices once a week can help you to rebalance the energy of your manipura chakra. By drinking only juice for one day, you will take advantage of one of nature's greatest healing agents. Juice fasting enhances your health and vigour. It gives your digestive system a rest, allowing your body to cleanse itself thoroughly.

Juice fasting makes your body and mind feel lighter. It also lowers your ego's defence mechanisms so that you are open to positive inspiration. It prepares your body and mind to absorb higher energy vibrations and to be more fully conscious. It assists you in developing healthy attitudes of self-confidence, will-power and mental resolve.

Once-a-week juice fast

It is best to choose a day when you don't have to work, when you can be as quiet as possible, perhaps at the weekend. You can return to your normal diet the next day.

Drink 2–3 litres (3½–5½ pints) of freshly made juice on your fast day. It is most beneficial, when you make the drink yourself, to use no more than three fruits or vegetables at a time. Don't mix fruits and vegetables in the same juice. Carrots, fresh ginger root and cabbage are particularly useful for stimulating a cleansing and balancing of the manipura energy. Don't use fleshy fruits, such as bananas or avocados.

Don't consume solid food, dairy products, caffeine or fizzy drinks during the fast. Avoid tea and coffee, but herbal teas, especially peppermint, are helpful. Drink plenty of water to flush out your system. If you experience a headache or nausea, drink hot water with a little lemon juice.

Use your time for quiet activity. Meditate as much as possible and try to keep your focus inward. Practise yoga asanas and breathing exercises to enhance the benefits of the fast.

Caution: Do not attempt a juice fast, or any other kind of fast, if you are pregnant, if you have had an eating disorder or if you suffer from anaemia. It is a good idea to consult your doctor or health-care professional if you have any doubts.

A regular practice of fasting on water or juices can prove very cleansing to your physical body, as well as help you to balance the energy of the manipura chakra.

Manipura Relationships

When your manipura energy is unblocked and balanced, people are intuitively drawn to you. They can feel that you are a strong, yet sensitive person with a high level of personal integrity. However, you have to be careful that people don't connect with you because they want you to take care of them or to tell them what to do.

The solar plexus is the physical centre of your body; it is your point of gravitational balance. In Taoist tradition, manipura is known as your "hara" point – your centre of control, power and strength. This is the energy "antenna" that you use most often to connect with others in both casual and work-related relationships.

Manipura is the chakra where you store most of your emotional baggage. Another person may (knowingly or unknowingly) "push your button" and stimulate a reaction that is way out of proportion.

A healthy flow of energy at the manipura chakra enhances all inter-personal relationships

The manipura chakra is also the seat of your "gut feelings". It is the chakra most relied on by many entrepreneurs and business people. It may be functioning too well in many successful gamblers and con men.

Problems in manipura relationships

A too-open solar plexus means that you take on other people's feelings and emotions too easily. One that is tightly closed makes it difficult, even impossible, for you to empathize with others. Instead, when your energy gets blocked at the manipura, you experience frustration, anger and rage.

Many dysfunctional families relate via erratic and/or blocked manipura energy. Arguing and fighting become the accepted mode of behaviour. It may be important for you to start to become aware of how many such habits and beliefs you absorbed at an early age. For example, if your family did not consider it acceptable to express fear or experience pleasure, an energetic blockage may have been created between the manipura and the swadhisthana–muladhara chakras. This may cause you to express these feelings in an angry manner (anger is the "demon" who sits at your solar plexus).

People who want to control or drain you may attempt to connect at the solar plexus. Subtle-energy leeching mainly takes place here, so it is the chakra that requires the most attention and balancing. Some people have so much charisma that they are able to force you to open this chakra to their negativity. This may cause you to lose confidence in yourself and have feelings of low self-esteem.

A HEALTHY WORKING RELATIONSHIP

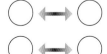

Communication at vishuddha (throat) chakra

Mutual flow of energy at manipura (solar plexus) chakra

Manipura Meditations

Meditation on your manipura chakra frees you from the need for the approval of others. It enables you to become calm, confident and to rely on your own inner resources. It enhances your appreciation of the visual beauty of nature, and it causes you to experience a greater connection with others and with the universe. Your mind and body become radiant, with a healthy glow to your skin and eyes.

Affirmations

Mentally repeat one or more of the following:

- I offer all my negative qualities to the fire of transformation.
- My enthusiasm enables me to achieve great things.
- I claim my personal power and accept responsibility for all areas of my life.
- My healthy appetite for the adventures of life enables me to digest its challenges with joy.
- My relationship with others is filled with courage, openness and confidence.

Meditation to transform anger

Repeat this meditation regularly, until you become aware that your behaviour is beginning to change in a positive way. Notice that you no longer feel irritation when faced with situations that previously would have stimulated your anger. Instead, you experience empathy, which is a positive energetic connection at the solar plexus level.

✪ Sit in a comfortable meditation position – do not lie down. Close your eyes and breathe gently through both nostrils. Rest your hands in your lap in the fire mudra (see picture, opposite) by making

THE MANIPURA CHAKRA

138

a fist of your right hand. Release your thumb so that it is pointing upward. Rest the right hand on the left in your lap, or on your thigh.

② Begin your meditation by remembering an incident that made you feel angry or irritated. For instance, you may have been in your car, late for an appointment and trying to find a place to park. Finally, you found a space, but someone else grabbed it first. Be aware of how you felt.

③ Allow yourself to re-live the incident just once or twice. Have a firm mental picture, but don't permit your mind to dwell on it.

④ Next change the image slightly. See yourself in the same situation, but instead of becoming angry, picture yourself remaining calm. Consciously let go of your anger.

⑤ Hold on to this positive mental image. Replay it in your mind several times.

Meditation using the fire mudra helps to maintain a healthy level of heat within your body and bodily functions, such as digestion.

Working with Manipura

The solar plexus chakra enables you to assimilate all that life has to offer. It is the "flywheel" that empowers and keeps all the other energetic wheels functioning smoothly.

The manipura chakra roughly corresponds to the Taoist concept of the hara point, which is particularly important in martial arts such as tai chi, akido and qigong, as well as in traditional Chinese medicine. It provides a focal point for many breathing and meditation techniques, as well as serving as your physical centre of balance and gravity.

Jathara parivritti – Reclining abdominal twist

1 Lie flat on your back with your legs together. Bend your knees and bring them up toward your chest. Hug your knees for a few seconds, breathing as deeply as possible.

2 When you are ready, place your left arm flat on the ground, straight out from your left shoulder, with your palm downward.

3 Place your right arm flat on the ground, straight out from your right shoulder, and twist to the right, until your knees are as close to the floor as possible. Be sure that both shoulders remain on the ground. Turn your head and look at your left hand, which is still stretched out at shoulder level. Hold the pose for 5–10 breaths.

4 Return to the centre and repeat on the other side.

Ardha-matsyendrasana – Half-spinal twist

1 Come into a kneeling position, sitting on your heels. Drop your hips to the floor on the left side of your feet.

2 Keeping your right knee (the top one) bent, place your right foot flat on the floor outside your left knee.

Jathara parivritti –
Reclining abdominal twist

Ardha-matsyendrasana –
Half-spinal twist

③ Stretch your left arm up; bring it over and around your right knee. Hold your right ankle with your left hand. If you can't reach, hold your left knee (the knee on the ground). Look over your right shoulder. Breathe deeply as you hold this pose for 10–30 seconds. With each exhalation, feel that you are going more deeply into it.

④ Release the position and repeat it on the other side.

Parivritta trikonasana – Rotated triangle

① Stand with your feet slightly more than shoulder width apart and parallel, with toes pointing straight ahead. Extend your arms out to the sides at shoulder height, with your elbows straight.

② Twist from your waist, rotating your upper body to face the right. Place your left hand on the floor outside your right foot. Use a block if you are unable to comfortably place your hand on the ground.

③ Stretch your right arm straight up and look up at your right hand. The fingers should be pointing up toward the ceiling. Hold the pose for at least 10 seconds, gradually increasing it to 30 seconds.

④ Stand up and repeat the pose on the other side.

Parivritta utkatasana – Seated awkward twist

① Sit on your heels, with your knees and feet together. Bring your palms flat against each other, just in front of your breastbone.

② Keeping your buttocks on your heels, rotate your upper body to face the left. Bring your right elbow down onto your left knee. Hold this position for 10–30 seconds.

③ Come back to the centre and repeat on the other side.

④ A more advanced variation of this pose is to bring your elbow onto the ground outside your opposite knee.

Other movements for manipura

Uddhyana bandha, dancing the Twist, Sufi dancing, sit-ups, laughing

Parivritta trikonasana – Rotated triangle

Parivritta utkatasana – Seated awkward twist

CHAPTER SEVEN

The Anahata Chakra

"In the heart there is a brilliant lotus,
endowed with divine glory."

Siva Samhita, 3.1

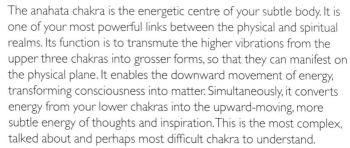

Anahata Chakra

The anahata chakra is the energetic centre of your subtle body. It is one of your most powerful links between the physical and spiritual realms. Its function is to transmute the higher vibrations from the upper three chakras into grosser forms, so that they can manifest on the physical plane. It enables the downward movement of energy, transforming consciousness into matter. Simultaneously, it converts energy from your lower chakras into the upward-moving, more subtle energy of thoughts and inspiration. This is the most complex, talked about and perhaps most difficult chakra to understand.

Your heart chakra enables you to express unselfish love and to be compassionate. It makes it possible for you to accept what life has to offer. With every breath your lungs draw in air, the element of the heart chakra. "Air" symbolizes all physical matter that is gaseous in form. Anahata energy does not repress or attempt to negate the emotions of the lower chakras. It sublimates them so you can express them in unselfish and unrestrained ways: love for love's sake.

Healing functions

The heart chakra governs your respiratory and circulatory systems. Asthma, bronchitis and lung cancer may be linked to anahata energy, as may pain in your ribs, upper back, shoulders, chest and thoracic spine. In women, this chakra is related to the health of the breasts.

ANAHATA BENEFITS

- Finding emotional balance

- Enhancing your ability in "heart-centred" activities

- Forgiving people who have harmed you

- Letting go of negativity

Vayou, Dieu du vent.

Mid-chest; thoracic region

Air, gas, breath, expansion, touch, contentment, peace, compassion, sympathy, kindness, love, joy, heart, balance, equanimity, devotion, bhakti, karma yoga, selfless service, grace, gratitude, put your heart into it, kind-hearted, big-hearted, warm heart, heart-felt, I give you my heart, her heart softened, his heart swelled with pride, have a heart

To consider the feelings of other people, love and be loved

Helps you to forge unselfish relationships

Self-acceptance, empathy, sympathy

Vayu, the god of air and winds, is pictured riding on an antelope, an animal said to be faster than the wind.

Using Anahata Chakra

Working with the energy of your anahata chakra can assist you in finding emotional balance in your life. It can enable you to let go of stress and negativity. And it can enhance your ability to form and maintain a loving partnership – or other "heart-centred" activities.

Tuning into the energy of your heart chakra enables you to forgive people who have harmed or slighted you in some way. Forgiving is quite different from forgetting or ignoring a wrong. It is the ability to observe and process your experience without getting caught up in reacting to it. With regular practice this process can free you from much emotional suffering.

On a physical level, letting go of negativity can improve your breathing patterns and your circulation. It can help to free you from many stress-related problems, including high blood pressure.

When to work with anahata energy

• You realize that you tend to be overly judgmental toward yourself.

• You would like to develop more compassion.

• You notice how painful it is to accept anything gracefully, even compliments.

• You feel an imbalance in your life: you are always the one who gives and serves others. It is seldom, if ever, reciprocated.

• You crave a loving partnership, but are unable to commit to or maintain one.

• You suffer from chronic respiratory problems, such as asthma.

• You have had a recent bereavement.

- How able am I to express my feelings "from the heart"?

- What could I do to initiate deep healing in my life?

- How might I include others in my healing process?

- Do I look to others to fulfil my emotional needs?

- What relationships that are "hanging in the air" do I need to release?

- Who must I forgive in order to be free?

- What do I need to forgive myself for?

- Do I tend to shy away from emotional intimacy?

Working with the anahata chakra can assist you in developing an attitude of loving kindness toward those in your life.

Symbolic Element and Energy

As you work with the energy of the anahata chakra, you develop the ability to create harmony and balance it in every aspect of your life. You learn to forgive yourself, as well as others. These teachings of the heart centre are symbolized by its various elements.

Meaning of name: anahata = un-struck – that is, subtle, non-physical sound. These are distinct from the sounds that you hear with your physical ears, which are produced by something hitting against something else.

Position: fourth from lowest chakra, in the thoracic (chest) region of your body, the mid-chest

Pattern of radiant energy: 12-petal lotus

Element: air = gaseous matter, wind

Geometric form representing air: two equilateral triangles superimposed on each other to form a six-pointed star

Symbolism of element: expansive in nature; you can feel air, but you can't see it

Mantra (seed sound) of element: YAM

Goals: Unselfish love, compassion, joy, balance, generosity, self-acceptance

Age of development: four–seven years

Consciousness: asking questions; sympathizing with the feelings of others; developing empathy

Female energy: Kakini is the most loving and helpful of the chakra guardians. Her energy prepares you to overcome all obstacles and to develop the power of deep concentration. In her four hands, she holds (1) a sword to enable you to cut through the obstacles blocking the upward movement of your energy; (2) a shield to protect you from external worldly conditions; (3) a skull, with which she cautions you to detach yourself from false identification with your physical body; and (4) a trident, to show that she keeps the three aspects of nature in balance.

Masculine custodian: Vayu, god of air and wind, is the regulator of your breath and the prana within your body. He is said to have developed the yoga practice of pranayama and taught it to his son Hanuman, the monkey god, who gave it to humanity.

Vayu roams the earth and rules the atmosphere. He is seated on an antelope and is often referred to as "the bearer of perfumes".

Animal: antelope or gazelle, animals who move like the wind. Sometimes a dove (another "air" animal) is pictured.

Positive emotions: caring, loving, giving

Negative emotions: grief, sorrow, sadness, envy, being heart-broken

Predominant sense: touch

Basic activity: manual work, including keyboarding or typing; grasping. The heart also controls the minor chakras in the hands.

Aspect of life force that has its headquarters in anahata chakra: vyana – the energy that enables nutrients (from food, breath, ideas and beauty) to be transported to where they are needed.

The geometric form of the anahata chakra is composed of two superimposed equilateral triangles, symbolizing balance.

Meditating on Anahata Yantra

1 Place a picture of the anahata chakra on your meditation table, slightly below your eye level. Sit in a comfortable, meditative position and look directly at the picture with your eyes half-closed.

2 First gaze at the upper right-hand corner of the yantra, at approximately "one o'clock". Then begin to slowly rotate your eyes clockwise around the circumference of the picture.

3 Notice the 12 brick-red petals with Sanskrit mantras: KAM, DHAM, GAM, GHAM, NYAM, CHAM, CHHAM, JAM, JHAM, JNAM, TAM, THAM. These 12 mantras represent qualities that meditation on the anahata yantra will help you to get rid of: lustfulness, fraudulence, indecision, repentance, hopelessness, anxiety, longing, impartiality, arrogance, incompetence, discrimination and an attitude of defiance.

4 After several rounds, allow your eyes to spiral inward to look at the black antelope or gazelle. He is an animal who is as swift as the wind and as restless as air. On his back, the antelope carries a smoky-grey, six-pointed star. This star-mandala, often referred to as the "Star of David", is made up of two intersecting equilateral triangles. The upward-pointing triangle is symbolic of Siva, consciousness, the passive masculine energy. The downward-pointing triangle represents Shakti, the active, creative female energy. Your heart chakra is the meeting point of these two currents.

At the centre of the star is the Sanskrit mantra "YAM", the seed mantra for Vayu. He is the guardian spirit of air, the element of the anahata chakra.

5 You are now at the energetic centre of the yantra. Try to hold your concentration there, preferably on the bindu, the dot at the top of the "YAM".

Anahata Imbalances

When the energy at your heart chakra is balanced and free of blockages you rarely feel lonely. You are not lacking in the ability to forgive, nor are you short of sympathy. You would not be the type of person who would stay in a loveless marriage. Also you would be unlikely to deny yourself proper medical care or physical nurturing. People with imbalances in their heart chakras are often referred to as "hard-hearted" or as suffering from a "tightening of the heart".

What to look for

Grief, sorrow, jealousy, passiveness, heartache, difficulty in giving and/or receiving love, loneliness and depression. Physical conditions that may indicate an imbalance of anahata energy include shallow breathing, respiratory congestion, asthma, lung diseases, breast cancer, recurring bouts of pneumonia, chronic upper back pain, high blood pressure and physical heart problems.

Working to unblock anahata energy enables you to be caring and sympathetic. Your relationships become less selfish in nature; you begin to develop the ability to both give and receive kindness.

Possible causes of imbalances

You may be suffering from unresolved sorrow, perhaps someone you loved died and you were unable to grieve sufficiently. Maybe your marriage (or the marriage of your parents) ended in a painful divorce. You may have experienced rejection, withdrawal of love or abandonment. Perhaps you loved someone "whole-heartedly" and they abused you, either physically or emotionally.

Often imbalances at the heart chakra are connected to emotions that tried to find a healthy expression in your lower chakras, but were distorted. This may be because your family disapproves of emotions and demands that you keep your feelings in check.

THE ANAHATA CHAKRA

WHEN ANAHATA ENERGY IS EXCESSIVE

• You may be involved in a co-dependent relationship.

• You tend to take on the problems of others.

• The woes of the world affect you too deeply.

• You have a tendency to "smother" your children with affection.

• You give too much and too frequently, often neglecting your own needs.

• You fall in love too quickly and are easily hurt.

• You are an "air-head" – the excess of the quality of airiness makes you forgetful.

• You have difficulty in sticking to things.

WHEN ANAHATA ENERGY IS DEFICIENT

• You feel lonely and isolated – even when you are physically with other people.

• You have trouble sustaining a healthy, loving relationship – or may find it impossible to commit to one.

• You lack sympathy for others.

• You are bitter and overly critical.

• You are a passive-aggressive.

• You are selfish and unable to give. It is especially difficult for you to give of yourself.

• You are miserly with your energy.

• You feel "heavy-hearted".

ENERGY EXERCISE

Balancing Anahata Energy

This mudra helps you to rebalance the energy of your heart chakra and stimulates its gradual emotional cleansing. Practise it whenever your feel drained, exploited or misunderstood. It is especially helpful during times of loneliness and despair. The lotus mudra aids you in opening yourself up to the divine will and allowing yourself to receive whatever it is that you really need. If you practise it on a regular basis, it assists you in finding unconditional love, good will, genuine affection and loving communication.

The blossoming lotus represents your heart opening. The flower is firmly rooted in the "mud" of the lower chakras, but it is adamant in its resolve to grow upward toward the light – the knowledge of the higher centres. The lotus is a symbol of your inner beauty emerging from the darkness. You can use the lotus mudra in conjunction with the loving-kindness meditation (see pages 160–61).

Lotus mudra

① Bring your palms together at your chest, with the fingers vertical and relaxed.

② Keeping the fingertips and the bases of the hands together, bend your fingers slightly and bow your knuckles outward. Notice how they now resemble the bud of a lotus flower.

③ Keeping the tips of the little fingers and the outside edges of the thumbs together, slowly separate the other fingers and spread them out wide. This represents the opening of the heart chakra.

④ Take four to five deep breaths as you mentally repeat the affirmation, "I open my heart to receive whatever comes my way."

⑤ Then slowly bring your fingertips back into the "bud" position. Repeat this several times.

Lotus mudra

2

3

Anahata Relationships

When your anahata energy is unblocked and balanced, you are able to relate to others in an unselfish way. You can establish and maintain caring relationships that include the ability to receive love, as well as to give it.

The concept of a loving, giving person who never takes anything for him or herself is not a healthy one energetically. It is like a person who always exhales, but never takes the time to inhale properly. After a while, there is nothing left to give. If you are a person who always gives from the heart, but feels guilty about receiving love, perhaps it important to take the time to restore a mutually nourishing balance to your relationships.

Letting go

Your anahata chakra is what enables you to let go of relationships that no longer exist. When a loved one dies or a loving relationship ends, the energy of your anahata chakra goes out of balance. You may still be giving the energy out, but there is no one to receive and return it. It probably feels as though your energy is dissipating into airy nothingness.

Sorrow is an experience of inner airiness or emptiness. It is important to give yourself the time and the permission to grieve properly. This will restore the healthy flow of energy at your anahata chakra.

Relationships involving the energy of the heart chakra are strongly connected to your ability to express the emotions of your lower chakras. If these are distorted for some reason, you may have difficulty in establishing healthy long-term loving relationships. Perhaps you come from a family or a society that disapproves of the open display of emotions and they demand that you keep your feelings in check. This would strongly affect the expression and energetic balance of your heart chakra. Or perhaps you have been trained from childhood (as most women are) to always give – this would deplete your anahata energy. It is not possible to always be giving and never receiving, any more than it is possible to always exhale without allowing yourself to inhale.

A HEALTHY, LOVING PARTNERSHIP

 Communication at vishuddha (throat) chakra

 Mutual flow of energy at anahata (heart) chakra

LOSS OF SOMEONE YOU LOVE

 Death of a loved one or final breakup of a relationship leaves you feeling empty and airy; there is no one to return your energy.

YOU ARE A PERSON WHO IS ALWAYS GIVING

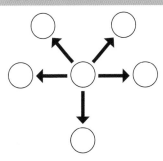 The central circle represents you. The outer circles might stand for your partner, children, parents, friends and/or work colleagues.

Anahata Meditations

Meditation on your anahata chakra frees you from the idea that matter in gaseous form (such as air) is real. You gain mastery over your sense of touch and over the activity of giving/receiving. Your mind becomes expansive in nature.

Affirmations

Mentally repeat one or more of the following, as you envision a positive change (for example, a breath of fresh air):

• I forgive myself.

• I forgive [insert name of a person you feel has wronged you in some way] and am grateful for the lesson that s/he taught me.

• My heart is free of unnecessary burdens.

• I experience great joy and therefore have great energy.

• My spirit is as boundless and free as the air.

Loving-kindness meditation

If you practise this simple but powerful meditation on a regular basis, you may experience a healing of past traumas along with associated emotional releases. Memories of past grief may come to mind. Be easy and nurturing with yourself. You may want to end your meditation by repeating the Sanskrit mantra "Lokah samasta sukhino bhavantu" meaning "May all beings everywhere be happy and free."

1 Sit in a comfortable meditative position. Close your eyes and bring your awareness to the centre of your chest. Take a few deep breaths and then let your breath find its natural rhythm.

2 Visualize your heart as an unopened rose. As you concentrate on it, the bud slowly begins to open and you feel your heart opening

with it. Notice the healing warmth that radiates out from your heart centre. Feel it instilling a sense of general well-being into every part of your body.

③ To assist the heart-opening progress, mentally repeat the phrases: "May I be happy. May I be healthy. May I live with ease. May I be free of dis-ease." It is important to begin with self-healing.

④ When you feel ready, picture the face of someone you care about. It may be a friend or a family member. Feel their presence and then direct the phrases of loving kindness to them. "May [insert name] be happy. May [insert name] be healthy."

⑤ Next, call to mind someone you know who is going through a difficult period. Imagine the warmth of your heart radiating out to this person. Mentally repeat, "May [insert name] be happy. May [insert name] be healthy. May [insert name] live with ease."

⑥ Finally, think of a person you consider to have injured you in some way. Feel your heart communicating compassion to that person. Mentally repeat "May [insert name] be happy. May [insert name] be free of dis-ease."

Using the chin mudra for meditation invites calmness and helps you to tune in to a new awareness. To make this mudra, bring the tip of your thumb to the tip of the index finger to form a circle. Relax the other fingers.

Working with Anahata

Your heart chakra is the energetic centre of your body. If you are not balanced in your breathing in and your breathing out, it will be difficult for you to maintain your mental poise. Similarly, although you have been told "It is better to give than receive", always giving is not possible. You need to receive energy in order to be able to give it.

Namaskar – Prayer position

Bring your palms together directly in front of your breastbone. This is the classic position for prayer. It assists you in centring both your body and your mind. In Indian tradition, this hand position is used as a gesture of greeting, indicating "My soul meets your soul".

Urdhva-mukhaswanasana – Upward-facing dog pose

1 Lie on your abdomen; place your hands flat on the ground under your shoulders.

2 Straighten your arms, allowing your chest, hips and legs to lift off the ground, until you are resting only on the tops of your feet and your hands. Make sure that your knees and elbows are straight. Hold this position for 10–30 seconds as you breathe deeply.

Ustrasana – Camel pose

1 Sit on your heels. It is best to have your knees and feet together, but you may separate them slightly, if necessary. Lift your body so that you are now standing on your knees.

2 Reach back with your right hand and catch hold of your right heel. Then reach with your left hand to hold onto your left heel.

3 Let your head drop back. Lift your hips up and forward as much as possible. Feel your breastbone arching upward. Breathe deeply as you hold the pose for 10 seconds, gradually increasing the time

Namaskar –
Prayer position

Urdhva-mukhaswanasana –
Upward-facing dog pose

Ustrasana –
Camel pose

to 30 seconds. Come down and relax with your forehead on the ground. Repeat the camel pose two to three times.

Dhanruasana – Bow pose
① Lie on your abdomen. Separate your legs, bend your knees and bring your feet up. Reach back and take hold of your ankles.

② Keep your elbows straight. Inhale as you lift your head, chest and legs off the ground. Lift your legs as high as possible. Breathe and hold the position for as long as you feel comfortable.

Caution: Never attempt the bow pose if you are pregnant.

Chakrasana – Wheel pose
① Lie flat on your back with your knees bent and your feet flat on the ground. Try to have your feet parallel to each other and as close to your buttocks as possible. Place your hands flat on the ground behind your shoulders, with fingers pointing in toward your body.

② Lift your hips, then your chest. Straighten your arms and arch upward. Only your hands and feet are now on the ground. Breathe deeply as you hold the position for as long as you feel comfortable.

Gomukhasana – Cow's head pose
① Sit on your heels with knees and feet together. Bend your left elbow and bring it behind your back. Bend your right arm and bring the elbow up, with your hand hanging down. Clasp your hands behind your back. If you can't reach, use a strap or small towel to hold on to instead. Breathe as you hold the pose for 10–30 seconds.

② Change arms and repeat on the other side.

Other movements for anahata
Jumping jacks, hugging, prayer, yoga breathing exercises, acts of random kindness, selfless service

Dhanruasana –
Bow pose

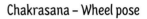

Chakrasana – Wheel pose

Gomukhasana –
Cow's head pose

CHAPTER EIGHT

The Vishuddha Chakra

"At the base of the throat is the
Vishuddha chakra, where the goddess
of speech resides."

Sir John Woodroffe, *The Serpent Power*

Vishuddha Chakra

The vishuddha chakra is the communication centre of your subtle body. It enables you to listen deeply, as well as to speak with conviction. If its energy is out of balance it impedes communication between your heart and mind. It may block the feelings that arise in your heart; you may not think them through properly and may act too impulsively or irrationally. When your throat chakra is open, the ideas, hopes and dreams that come from your ajna chakra can be "taken to heart".

At your throat chakra the energy is one of language, not emotions. Vishuddha can express blessings and sweet words. But it can also enable you to articulate too much negativity if you are feeling blocked, so it is important to keep its energy pure and open.

Healing functions

In your physical body, the throat chakra governs your neck, throat, oesophagus, thyroid and parathyroid glands, vocal chords, trachea, cervical spine (the seven vertebrae in your neck), mouth, teeth and gums, hypothalamus, tonsils, ears and auditory system. As your communication centre, it gives you energy to hear and speak.

When its energy is blocked, you may be prone to frequent sore throats, speech impediments, eating disorders, deafness, tightness of jaw, teeth clenching or a thyroid imbalance.

VISHUDDHA BENEFITS

- Improving your communication and creativity
- Strengthening skills such as public speaking, singing or dancing
- Developing your inner voice
- Making your voice, face and body more expressive

LOCATION

Throat

KEYWORDS

Communication, voice, speech, silence, ether/ akasha, sky, space, hearing, artistic, creative, imagination, innovative, swallow, silver tongue, body language, hunger and thirst

ASPIRATIONS

To communicate your feelings, express yourself in healthy, positive ways, understand others

WORKING WITH VISHUDDHA

Develops your creative abilities

ENHANCES

Self-expression, compassionate listening and deep communication

Indra, king of the gods, and the elephant he rides, are both symbolic of the vishuddha chakra.

Using Vishuddha Chakra

Working with the energy of your vishuddha chakra can assist you in improving your communication skills and artistic creativity. It can give you an easy command of language and the ability to compose poetry, to be a good listener, to understand dreams and to be a good teacher (especially a spiritual teacher).

Communication involves listening as well as speaking. Notice whether you are listening with your ego (ajna), your emotions (anahata) or a balance of the two.

Freeing your throat chakra may involve strengthening your physical communication skills through public speaking, singing, dance or story-telling. It may also involve developing your inner voice

The freedom of expression that comes when the energy of your vishuddha chakra is balanced enhances all aspects of your life.

through journal-writing or painting. On a physical level, working with your throat chakra gives you a clear, strong, sweet voice. It also makes your face and body more expressive.

When to work with vishuddha energy

• You have trouble expressing what you know/believe to be right.

• People complain that you tend to dominate conversations.

• When you are with other people, you can't think of anything to say, so you just sit and listen.

• You feel as though your self-expression is being stifled.

• You are prone to gossip.

• You have a speech impediment.

• You suffer from an eating disorder.

• You are stressed.

VISHUDDHA JOURNALING — SUGGESTED QUESTIONS

• What aspects of myself am I unwilling to hear the truth about?

• Do I live my "truth"?

• Do my thoughts, words and actions agree?

• Am I shy about speaking up because I'm afraid to make a scene?

• Do I tend to dominate conversations?

• How often do I fail to keep my promises (including being late for appointments)?

• Do I use my words to hurt others or to try to empower them?

• How transparent are my motives?

• Do I often express my thoughts or feelings as being the "truth"?

• What unfinished communication might be creating obstacles in my life?

Symbolic Element and Energy

By working with the energy of your throat chakra, you become better able to communicate your thoughts, feelings, hopes and dreams – and to deeply "hear" what others have to say. All this is symbolized by the elements of the vishuddha chakra.

Meaning of name: vishuddha = purity

Position: fifth from lowest chakra, in region of your throat and laryngeal plexus

Pattern of radiant energy: 16-petal lotus

Element: ether = space

Geometric form representing ether: crescent moon

Symbolism of element: all-pervading; space can exist when no other elements are present

Mantra (seed sound) of element: HAM

Goals: deep communication and artistic development

Age of development: 7–12 years

Consciousness: communicating with others, rather than just talking or just listening

Female energy: Shakini, whose skin is the colour of pale-pink roses. As the guardian of the vishuddha chakra, she can open the door for you to receive the gifts of psychic powers, good memory, sharp wit and the ability to improvise. In her four hands she carries: (1) a skull to remind you to be detached from the illusions of the world; (2) a staff to control your memory; (3) a book representing the knowledge of right living; and (4) a string of beads that can be used as a centring device to free your mind from restlessness and constant internal chatter.

Masculine custodian: Indra, king of the devas (beings of light) controls thunder and rain. He leads the protectors of the other chakras in their never-ending battle against negativity – that is, your lower nature.

Animal: "Airavata", the mythological white elephant with seven trunks who is Indra's vehicle. He has the ability to move freely through time and space and is quite different from the heavy, black, earthbound elephant of the muladhara chakra.

Positive emotions: honesty, truthfulness, purity, being drawn to artistic inspiration and expression

Negative emotions: deceit, lies, shyness, writer's block. When communication is blocked, vishuddha becomes the seat of your addictions.

Predominant sense: hearing

Basic activity: speaking

Aspect of life force that has its headquarters in vishuddha chakra: udana, the energy that directs your aspirations upward and aids in the production of unique sound – that is, your voice

Working with your vishuddha chakra can help you to enhance your artistic expression as well as your spiritual practice.

Meditating on Vishuddha Yantra

① Place a picture of the vishuddha chakra on your meditation table, slightly below your eye level. Light a candle; you may choose to burn incense as well.

② Sit in a comfortable meditative position and close your eyes.

③ Take a few long, slow, deep breaths. Spend a few moments listening to the sound of your breath as it passes through your throat. When you are ready, open your eyes halfway and fix your gaze on the picture.

④ Begin by looking at the upper right hand, approximately halfway between "12 o'clock" and "one o'clock". Slowly rotate your eyes clockwise around the 16 lavender-purple petals.

⑤ Notice the Sanskrit letters written on the petal. Each represents a mantra that is derived from one of the 16 vowels of the Sanskrit alphabet, representing pure sounds. They are: AM, AAM, IM, EEM, UM, OOM, RIM, REAM, LIM, LEAM, EM, AIM, OM, AUM, AM, AH. Most of these mantras are associated with musical sounds. Meditation on vishuddha yantra enhances your appreciation of music and chanting. Vishuddha filters the impure energies from the five lower chakras; it distils them into untainted vibrations.

⑥ After several rounds, allow your eyes to spiral inward to look at the mythological white elephant with seven trunks. He is the vehicle of Indra, leader of the devas. Behind the elephant is a smoky-purple crescent moon, the symbol of "space", the physical element associated with the vishuddha chakra.

⑦ On his back, the elephant carries the Sanskrit mantra "HAM", the seed mantra for akasha (space). Try to hold your concentration on the bindu, the dot at the top of the "HAM".

Vishuddha Imbalances

When the energy at your throat chakra is balanced and unimpeded, your words are kind, thoughtful, clear and truthful. You use your speech to express yourself in a manner that is alive and pulsating with expression. Your voice is strong and vibrant. You tend to be at ease in writing, speaking and sharing your thoughts and feelings with others. You are able to listen to and express what is in your heart. You are as comfortable with silence as you are with speaking.

What to look for
The strongest indication that the energy of your vishuddha chakra is blocked or out of balance is that you have difficulty in communicating. Even if you are a creative person, you may suffer from writer's block from time to time.

Physical symptoms often include a raspy throat, hoarse voice, chronic sore throat, mouth ulcers, gum difficulties, laryngitis (loss of voice), swollen glands, thyroid problems, throat cancer, tonsillitis and frequent "lumps" in your throat when you try to speak. Blockages also manifest as eating disorders, addictions or speech impediments.

Possible causes of imbalances
Holding tension in your throat chakra is usually the result of repressed creativity or freedom of expression, especially during your formative years. As a child, you may have frequently cried yourself to sleep. Perhaps you grew up in an environment where people believed that "children should be seen but not heard". Maybe your attempts to communicate your thoughts or feelings were/are met with an admonition to "be quiet". Or you were a victim of authoritarianism, when you were punished if you "talked back"?

You might have been forced to keep secrets, blackmailed (especially emotionally), or fed lies and mixed messages. Many families shout instead of talking to each other. Perhaps you suffered from verbal abuse or excessive criticism.

Very loud music, sounds of violent video games and violence on television all contribute to vishuddha imbalances. Constant background noise unbalances the energy of your throat chakra and makes your connection to inner silence difficult.

WHEN VISHUDDHA ENERGY IS EXCESSIVE

• You talk too much, often without having anything substantial to say.

• You gossip frequently.

• You always have to have the last word and tend to not listen to what others have to say.

• You shout rather than speak.

• Your voice is too loud or too authoritarian.

• Your artistic output may be extensive, but lacks authentic inspiration.

• You have difficulty in paying attention because you think you already know it all.

WHEN VISHUDDHA ENERGY IS DEFICIENT

• You are timid and scared to express yourself.

• You are afraid to speak and/or sing in public.

• You over-react to loud sounds.

• Your voice may be too soft, whiney or crack frequently, or you may speak in a monotone.

• You seem unsure of what you are saying.

• You stutter or have some other speech impediment.

• You are hearing-impaired or tone deaf.

• Your vocabulary is limited; you may have difficulty in learning foreign languages or playing a musical instrument.

Balancing Vishuddha Energy

This breathing exercise balances the energy of your throat chakra. It is a wonderful practice if you are a singer, teacher, need to speak in public or just want to improve your communication skills.

The humming breath improves your concentration, memory and confidence. Your desire to gossip vanishes. You will find yourself better able to listen deeply, as well as being able to communicate on a more profound level. It frees your mind from "chatter", prepares you to discover your own inner voice and it makes your voice sweet and melodious. If you are prone to throat problems, such as hoarseness or a weak voice, regular practice will probably improve these conditions.

The humming breath

1 Sit in a comfortable meditation position. Close your ears with your thumbs to make your inner silence more profound. Keeping your mouth and lips gently sealed, tighten the glottis at the back of your throat. Remember to keep your head erect and relax your neck muscles.

2 Inhale strongly through both of your nostrils, vibrating the soft palate and making a snoring sound. The snoring inhalation energizes your throat. Some people describe this as the sound you make when you are trying to clear your throat. Yoga scriptures liken it to the buzzing of a large black bumblebee.

3 Hold your breath for a few moments, for as long as you feel comfortable, focusing on your throat. It is during this slight retention that your mind experiences the elemental nature of the throat chakra: ether or space.

4 When you are ready to exhale, do so with a high-pitched hum. It should sound like the buzzing of a small honeybee. Try to exhale all the air in your lungs. Humming as you breathe out helps you to regulate your breath and makes for a longer exhalation. Repeat this exercise three to five times. Be aware of the feel of the vibration in your throat, mouth, cheeks, lips and sinus cavities.

Closing your ears to external sounds enhances the effects of the humming.

Vishuddha Relationships

When your vishuddha energy is unblocked and balanced, you are able to communicate with others in an honest and open manner. You are able to recognize and freely express your truths, creativity and emotional needs, without fear of what others might think. You are able to fully communicate with others, as deep listening is also linked to the energy of the throat chakra.

When the throat chakra is blocked, your communication may become distorted; you might lie without realizing it. For instance, you might be in the habit of putting on a "brave face" rather than attempting to express an inner turmoil or dissatisfaction. This would result in unexpressed emotions and stuck creativity.

Working to balance the energy of your vishuddha chakra can help you to develop authentic relationships involving deep communication.

HEALTHY GIVE AND TAKE

This represents a healthy exchange of energy at the vishuddha (throat) chakra

BLOCKAGE OF VISHUDDHA ENERGY

Here one person is talking down or attempting to manipulate the other, causing the vishuddha energy to be blocked.

WHEN SELF-EXPRESSION IS SUPPRESSED

If you were brought up in a situation where you were told to "be quiet" when you attempted to express yourself, it probably caused a tightening of the throat chakra, as well as diminished energy flowing at both your anahata (heart) chakra (seat of love and compassion) and your manipura (solar plexus) chakra (seat of your self-image). Note that the person who seems to have a lot of energy is actually him/herself blocked at the vishuddha (throat) chakra.

This represents a passive-aggressive person who speaks softly, but strongly sucks the energy from others.

Vishuddha Meditations

When you concentrate on balancing your vishuddha chakra, you achieve great success in life. Your enjoyment of reading and listening to good music is enhanced; you discover how to tap into your own artistic potential. You seem to have enough time for what you want to do.

Affirmations

Mentally repeat one or more of the following:

- I receive intuitive guidance and have the courage to act on it.
- My creative instincts are sound and pure.
- I always speak the truth. My word is my bond.
- My relationships with others are honest and straightforward.
- I communicate my feelings and emotions in healthy ways.
- I strive to understand, as well as to be understood.

SO HAM meditation – listening to the sound of your breath

Don't try to repeat the mantras, but listen to your breath as it naturally says them. Gradually your mind will calm. If your mind drifts off, keep bringing it back to your breath. This is your most natural focal point for attention because it is the universal obstacle to deep attention.

✪ Sit in a comfortable meditation position, preferably cross-legged. Make sure that you back is straight and your head erect. Rest the backs of your hands on your thighs. Join the tip of your thumb with the middle finger of the same hand. This is known as akasha mudra.

2 Give yourself the mental suggestion that you will sit still and be fully focused for the next 20–30 minutes. Try not to move a single muscle, or your mind will be drawn outward.

3 Close your eyes and bring your awareness to your breath. Take three to four deep breaths and then let go. Don't try to control your breath, instead concentrate on listening to its natural sound.

4 As you inhale, listen to your breath; hear it repeating the sound "SO". Feel your breath joyously drawing in life.

5 As you exhale, hear your breath repeating the mantra of the vishuddha chakra "HAM". Release pent-up tensions and aggressions. Let go of expectations. Be still and be open to the experience.

Akasha mudra, relating to the element of space, is an excellent way to relieve feelings of heaviness or congestion.

Working with Vishuddha

The vibration of the vishuddha chakra determines how and what you communicate. This includes spoken words, body language and the sound of silence. Emotions that arise in your lower chakras are expressed by the energy of your throat centre, as are your thoughts, dreams and hopes that originate in the two highest chakras.

Sarvangasana – Shoulderstand

It is best to follow the shoulderstand with the fish pose (see page 120). You may find that hormonal imbalances are helped by working with both the throat and sacral chakras.

1 Lie on your back with your legs together. Bring your hands onto your buttocks and slowly walk them down your back. Lift yourself up as straight as possible. Try to have your hands flat on your back, with your fingers pointing in toward your spine.

2 Consciously relax your calf muscles and your feet. If you are a beginner, hold this position for no more than 10 seconds. More advanced practitioners may stay for up to 3 minutes.

3 To come down, drop your legs halfway to the ground; bring your hands flat on the floor behind your back. Keep your head down as you slowly unroll your body.

Simhasana – The lion

1 Sit on your heels with your knees and feet together. Rest your hands on your thighs.

2 Inhale deeply and exhale strongly through your mouth. As you exhale, "spring" forward like a lion about to jump on its prey: straighten your arms, stiffen your body, make "claws" of your fingers,

Simhasana –
The lion

Sarvangasana –
Shoulderstand

Neck stretch – Back and forward

1

2

stick your tongue out as far as possible and bulge your eyes (roaring is optional). Then sit back on your heels and relax for a moment; repeat two to three times.

Neck stretches
These may be done sitting or standing.

Back and forward: ❶ Lift your chin as much as you can; visualize the back of your head touching your spine (see page 185).

❷ Then drop your head toward your breastbone. Repeat three to four times in each direction, then return your head to upright.

Side to side: ❶ Stretch your head to the right, trying to touch your right shoulder with your right ear. Do not allow your neck to twist or your shoulders to lift.

❷ Then stretch to the left. Repeat these movements three to four times in each direction.

Turn your head from side to side: Without moving your shoulders, turn your head to look over your right shoulder. Then turn to the left. Repeat these movements three to four times in each direction. (Exercise not illustrated.)

Taoist thyroid-strengthener
❶ Kneel with your buttocks resting on your heels. Tuck your toes under and place your hands flat on your back in the kidney region.

❷ Slowly arch your upper body back as you take a deep breath. Keep your buttocks on your heels.

❸ Exhale as you round your back and bend forward with your head and chest. Repeat these movements 10–12 times. Then rest with your forehead on the ground.

Other movements for vishuddha
Singing, chanting, humming, acting, toning, laughing yoga

Neck stretch – Side to side

1

2

Taoist thyroid-strengthener

2

3

CHAPTER NINE

The Ajna Chakra

"I think that contemplation on the space between the eyebrows is the best way to experience a blissful state. This is a suitable way to meditate, even if you are a person without extensive training. Its practice enables you to quickly become absorbed in the Infinite."

Swatmarama, *Hatha Yoga Pradipika*, 4.80

INTRODUCING
Ajna Chakra

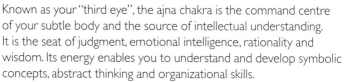

Known as your "third eye", the ajna chakra is the command centre of your subtle body and the source of intellectual understanding. It is the seat of judgment, emotional intelligence, rationality and wisdom. Its energy enables you to understand and develop symbolic concepts, abstract thinking and organizational skills.

Ajna chakra is your "sixth sense", which manages your five physical senses. It regulates the five lower chakras and the nadis (meridians) leading into them. Six spiritual powers are associated with your ajna chakra: the ability to control your thoughts and to direct your attention, perfect concentration, unobstructed meditation, enlightenment and samadhi (the super-conscious state).

Healing functions

In your physical body, the ajna governs your brain. On a more subtle level, its energy is related to the functioning of your mind. When the energy of your "third eye" is out of balance, physical symptoms may include headaches and poor eyesight. In extreme cases you may suffer a brain haemorrhage or a stroke, a tumour, Alzheimer's disease or epileptic seizures. You may have a learning disability or dyslexia, lack concentration, have frequent nightmares or be very forgetful. Many mental illnesses, such as schizophrenia and obsessive-compulsive disorder, also seem to be related to ajna imbalances.

AJNA BENEFITS

- Enhancing intuition

- Cultivating creativity and imagination

- Flexibility in opinions and viewpoints

- Breaking through to higher consciousness

The Siva and Shakti of Indian mythology represent opposing forces of nature that are now united.

LOCATION

Mid-forehead; between the eyebrows

KEYWORDS

Abstract thinking, perception, intuition, intellect, imagination, cognition, clairvoyance, discernment, focused mind, mental discipline, symbols, judgment, insight, sixth sense

ASPIRATIONS

To see the "big picture", such as a vision of your greater purpose in life

WORKING WITH AJNA

Develops your intuition, concentration and memory

ENHANCES

Balancing rational and logical thought with intuitive non-linear thought; deep communication

Using Ajna Chakra

Your ajna chakra is where perception meets logic; it is the highest expression of human polarity. By working with the energy of your brow centre, you can enhance your intuition and get a clearer insight into your purpose in the world. If your ajna energy is flowing well, you cultivate being a creative, imaginative person who has the ability to think symbolically as well as literally. You welcome new ways of looking at the world – and you are not afraid of changing your opinions and viewpoints.

It is here, at the brow chakra, that you need to make the third and final breakthrough to higher consciousness. The brow centre

The right side of the divine hermaphrodite holds a trident, the symbol of Siva. The left side represents the feminine aspect, known as Shakti

is the seat of the energetic knot of ego-awareness and intellectual pride. You must untie the knot at the ajna chakra to allow your spiritual energy to transcend duality. Your brow chakra must be freed and the energy flow unblocked before you can achieve the ultimate cosmic awareness.

This chakra is associated with an intuitive type of knowing. As you work with your ajna chakra, you may become clairvoyant or develop other psychic abilities.

Dreamwork

Your dreams offer a good way to connect with the ajna chakra. See page 201 for a guide to remembering your dreams and using them to balance and better relate to this chakra.

When to work with ajna energy

• You feel you could use more inspiration in your life.

• You are thinking about making major changes in your life, especially ones that would bring you more in line with your spiritual goals.

• You would like to be more focused.

• You hope to enhance your psychic potential.

• You need encouragement in your professional life.

AJNA JOURNALING — SUGGESTED QUESTIONS

• Do I tend to set my standards too high?

• Do I want my life to be better, but seem unable to imagine how to accomplish it?

• What are my long-term goals in life?

• Are my head and my heart in agreement?

• Is this my ego speaking or is this really the best action for me?

Symbolic Element and Energy

Working with your brow centre enables you to gradually free yourself from various self-imposed limitations and to see the "bigger picture" in life. The symbolic elements of the ajna chakra represent the union of the two aspects of your being.

Meaning of name: a = not; jna (nasal sound) = knowledge. It is interesting to note that your mind, which you probably view as your seat of wisdom, is here described as "not-knowledge". This is because (in philosophical terms) the ajna chakra is where you perceive yourself as being separate from the rest of the world – that is, your source of duality (see page 204 for a fuller description of this concept).

Position: the sixth from lowest chakra, at the point between your eyebrows

Pattern of radiant energy: two pure-white petals that make the chakra look a bit like a winged seed

Element: mind

Geometric form representing your mind: transparent luminous globe

Symbolism of element: beyond all physical elements

Mantra of element: OM

Goals: self-reflection; self-understanding

Age of development: adolescence

Consciousness: capable of abstract thinking; intuitive understanding; able to relate to symbolic concepts

Animal: instead of an animal, we see Ardhineshwara in the ajna chakra. This is the divine hermaphrodite, representing the mystical union of Siva and Shakti together in one body. The right (male) side of the body is ash grey and the left (female) side is pale pink.

Female energy: Shakti, on the left side, is the active creative power of the universe. She has two left arms. In one hand, Shakti holds a lotus flower, the symbol of beauty, purity and knowledge. In her other hand she holds a branch of sugar cane, which symbolizes the sweetness of life.

Masculine custodian: Siva, on the right, is pure consciousness; the passive eternal witness. He has two right arms. In one hand, Siva holds a trident representing the three aspects of consciousness: cognition, striving and attitude. His other hand is upraised in a gesture that is meant to dispel your fear.

Positive emotions: rationality, disciplined imagination

Negative emotions: self-righteousness, paranoia, anxiety, obsessions, hallucinations, cynicism, denial of reality

Predominant sense: intuition

Basic activity: thinking

Aspect of life force that has its headquarters in ajna chakra: prana – the energy that enables you to take in energy, nourishment and ideas

Working with the ajna chakra enhances your ability to see the "bigger picture" in all situations.

Meditating on Ajna Yantra

1 Place a picture of the ajna chakra on your meditation table, slightly below your eye level. Notice that it comprises a luminescent white circle with a pure-white petal on each side.

2 Light a candle; you may choose to burn incense as well. Sit in a comfortable meditative position.

3 Begin by looking at the petal to the right of the inner circle. The Sanskrit letter KSHAM is written on it. This represents the end of the subtle energy channel, known as the ida. Although when you look at the picture, you view it as being on the right, it is actually connected to the left side of your body, which is controlled by the right hemisphere of your brain, whose functions are intuitive, simultaneous, spatial, non-verbal, subjective, emotional and holistic.

4 After some time, move your eyes clockwise to the other lotus petal. On it is the Sanskrit mantra HAM, associated with pingala, your "masculine" qualities. It is connected to the right side of your body and the left hemisphere of your brain, whose functions are logical, sequential, mathematical, verbal, objective, rational and analytical.

5 Now move to the picture of Ardhineshwara, half man, half woman. His right side is the masculine Siva, representing passive consciousness. On his left side is Shakti, the feminine active creative principle.

6 In the central circle of the yantra is the Sanskrit mantra "OM", the source of all other mantras and the foundation of the universe itself. OM is the transcendental mantra of the ajna chakra; it represents "soundless sound", which cannot be heard with your physical ears. OM is the most abstract and the highest mantra. OM is the manifested symbol of the original vibration, the Divine Word, which caused the universe to come into being (the yogic Big Bang).

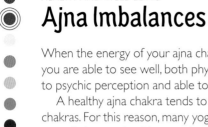

Ajna Imbalances

When the energy of your ajna chakra is unblocked and balanced, you are able to see well, both physically and intuitively. You are open to psychic perception and able to view the "bigger picture".

A healthy ajna chakra tends to encourage balance in the lower chakras. For this reason, many yogis suggest that it is best to begin your chakra work with your ajna chakra. Once your ajna chakra is balanced and free of blockages, it helps to counteract many negative effects that occur in your other chakras.

What to look for

You tend to be indecisive and jump to conclusions. You may be plagued by nightmares, migraine headaches, poor eyesight, lack of concentration or extensive forgetfulness.

Imbalances of the third eye often manifest physically as dizziness and endocrine imbalances. A misaligned brow chakra can be related to such problems as mental confusion, insomnia and acute sinusitis. It may lead you to be extremely self-righteous and excessively proud of your intellectual capacity. You might misuse your intellectual abilities. If the imbalance is very extreme, you may live in a world of illusion, suffer from hallucinations and have little or no connection with reality.

Possible causes of imbalances

A variety of traumas may cause imbalances of ajna energy. You might have witnessed something that was particularly ugly, brutal or frightening. You might have been betrayed by your spiritual teacher or someone whom you particularly looked up to. Perhaps you can't accept or are unable to "see" something that is vitally important to the growth of your soul.

THE AJNA CHAKRA

198

WHEN AJNA ENERGY IS EXCESSIVE

- You suffer from headaches, hallucinations, nightmares.

- You are so focused that your vision is narrow.

- You lack flexibility in thinking.

- You have a rigid, obsessive personality.

- You constantly evaluate yourself.

- You obsessively analyze every action and project negative outcomes.

- You have a holier-than-thou attitude and are overly conscientious.

- You suffer from delusions.

- You are too intellectual or detached from world.

- You lack the capacity to tune into your intuitive abilities – or you might not trust them. As a result, you tend to compensate by being highly logical, dogmatic, authoritarian and perhaps arrogant.

- You may have an over-abundance of intellectual capacity but are lacking in compassion.

WHEN AJNA ENERGY IS DEFICIENT

- You may have poor vision or other eye problems.

- You suffer from poor memory or tend to be foggy about details.

- You have difficulty in visualizing the outcome of your actions.

- You have difficulty in learning from your past experiences.

- You fear new ideas and new experiences.

- You lack self-discipline.

- You can't see things that are "as plain as the nose on your face".

- You are inclined to set your sights and your personal standards too low. This stems from your lack of inner vision and imagination.

Balancing Ajna Energy

Hakini mudra is a hand gesture that can be practised at any time and in any place. You may choose to do it whenever you feel the need to rebalance the energy of your ajna chakra. It helps you to remember things, connects you to sources of intuitive guidance and enhances your intellectual capacities. It does so by stimulating the communication between the right and left hemispheres of your brain and generating better cooperation between them.

This mudra is helpful whenever you are doing mental work. It is recommended for memory training and when undertaking management courses. Hakini mudra improves and deepens your respiration, benefitting your brain and recharging its energy.

Hakini mudra

1 Sit in any comfortable upright position, but don't cross your legs or ankles. If possible, it is helpful to sit facing east. Bring the tip of each finger to the tip of the respective finger on your other hand. The tips of your thumbs will be touching each other, as will the tips of the index fingers, and so on. You may have your eyes open or closed, but be sure to direct them upward toward your third eye.

2 Take 5–10 deep breaths. With each inhalation, bring the tip of your tongue onto your gums, just behind your upper front teeth. As you exhale, let your tongue relax. Your mind's eye will begin to see whatever it was that you wanted.

3 You can also use hakini mudra to concentrate on something for a longer period; practise it when you seek inspiration. After the initial 5–10 deep breaths, continue sit in deep contemplation with both hands in the mudra. Keep your eyes turned toward the centre of your forehead and the movement of your tongue synchronized with your breath – this will keep you from drifting off or falling asleep.

THE AJNA CHAKRA

Hakini mudra can be used at any time or place to help focus the energy of your ajna chakra.

DREAMWORK

- Understanding and analyzing your dreams can help you to balance and better relate to the energy of your ajna chakra. Place a notebook and pen next to your bed.

- At night, as you fall asleep, make a strong resolve that you will remember your dream(s).

- When you wake up, do not get out of bed immediately. Lying in bed, with your eyes closed, mentally review your dreams. Then sit up and write down as much as you can remember – even if it is not logical or in the correct order.

- Once you have the details of your dream on the page, think about the inner meaning as it relates to your life. Dreams are expressions of your being that have been freed from the logic of the physical world. In them your mind is able to express itself without being governed by mundane rules such as time, space and causation.

Ajna Relationships

Thought and sound manifest at four fundamental levels, with the audible sound of the vishuddha chakra at the gross physical end of the spectrum and transcendental "soundless" sound at the most subtle. Your ajna chakra represents your inner voice; it is an energetic antenna that enables you to relate to others on two levels:

- **Telepathic communication** This is the universal pre-language level of thought through which you look at or experience something without naming it.
- **Language** Most people's selection of words is filtered through a mental prism clouded by their native language, preconceptions, impressions, emotions and other limitations.

A healthy teacher–student relationship involves open communication and respect on both sides.

Communication through ajna

A good teacher–student relationship involves verbal speech, communicating words that express inner thoughts, as well as telepathic communication. Think about the best teachers you've ever had. What probably made those teachers so special was their ability to communicate not only verbally, but also their skill at conveying their own inner experiences.

Good teachers keep you focused and teach you how to balance the energy of your ajna chakra. Teachers who are speaking from experience are more likely to inspire you with their passion, give clear explanations with practical examples and make complicated things seem simple. They are also able to show you how things tie together.

Some people put up a barrier in an attempt to hide their thoughts and project a different image. In that case, no real communication takes place, even though the people seem to be speaking to each other.

A GOOD TEACHER–STUDENT RELATIONSHIP

 Understanding at ajna (brow) chakra

 Communication at vishuddha (throat) chakra

TRUE COMMUNICATION IS PREVENTED

 A barrier at the ajna (brow) chakra prevents real communication between two people

 Communication at vishuddha (throat) chakra

Ajna Meditations

The ajna chakra is identified with your mind and sense of individual self. Of all the chakras, the energy of the brow chakra has the most powerful overall effect on your personality. This is where you integrate your perception of the outer world to create your inner reality. Meditation on your ajna chakra frees you from the illusion that any cognitive perceptions are real. Your sense of separateness of body and mind disappears.

It is here, at your brow chakra, that you need to make the final "breakthrough" to higher consciousness. Once you break the energetic knot of ego-awareness and intellectual pride, your spiritual energy can transcend duality. Without letting go of your identification with your limited sense of self, you can go no further.

Affirmations

Sit in your preferred meditation position. Rest the backs of your hands on your thighs in the chin mudra: join the tips of your index finger and thumb on each hand. The remaining fingers are relaxed. Focus on the point between your eyebrows and mentally repeat one of the following affirmations:

• My mind is strong, focused and alert.

• I trust the inspirations of my higher self.

• I am self-disciplined yet sensitive to the needs of those around me.

Bhuchari – gaze into the void

Bhuchari stimulates your ajna chakra; it is a powerful psychic cleanser that greatly enhances your powers of concentration. If you wear glasses or contact lenses, it is best to remove them before you begin this meditation exercise.

① Sit in your preferred meditation position, preferably cross-legged, facing a white wall. Make sure that your spine is straight, head erect and your body relaxed.

② Bring the thumb of your right hand to the centre of your upper lip. Let your index, middle and ring fingers relax as you stretch your little finger straight forward. Stare at the tip of little finger with a steady gaze, trying not to blink. There should be no tension in this.

③ Your eyes will probably start to produce tears; this cleanses your eyes, tear ducts and sinuses. As well as strengthening your eyes and the nerve centres in your forehead, it is also a powerful psychic cleanser of the ajna chakra region and promotes intense concentration.

④ Practise this for 5 minutes. Then drop your hand and continue to gaze at the point where your index finger was.

⑤ Gaze at this void for at least 15–20 minutes every day.

Use bhuchari mudra to measure the distance of your gaze.

Working with Ajna

Your brow chakra controls your "vision" of the world, as well as your place in it. For example, as an adult, you probably have a fixed view of what the world "should look like", which makes poses like the headstand difficult. In reality, accomplishing it is little more than changing your point of view.

Sirsasana – Headstand

① Sit on your heels with your knees and feet together. Clasp hold of your elbows with opposite hands. Place your elbows on the ground directly beneath your shoulders. Without moving your elbows, release your hands and clasp them together by interlocking the fingers. Your forearms now form a "tripod" on the ground. When you practise the headstand with your arms in this position, the weight of your body is on your elbows rather than on your head or neck.

② Place the frontal portion of your head on the ground. Have the back of your head resting gently against your clasped hands. Straighten your knees without moving your head or elbows.

③ Slowly walk your feet forward until your hips are directly over your head. Don't allow your arms or head to move as you do this. Make sure that your weight remains on your elbows – don't allow it to come onto your head.

④ Bend your knees without letting your hips drop. Bring your heels up to your buttocks. Breathe deeply and hold this position for at least 10 seconds before going any further in attempting the full headstand.

⑤ When you feel comfortable, slowly bring your bent knees up toward the ceiling. Straighten your knees, lifting your feet. Have

THE AJNA CHAKRA

Sirsasana –
Headstand

your weight evenly balanced on your elbows. Breathe deeply and hold the position for as long as you feel comfortable. Be particularly aware of your relationship with gravity.

6 When you are ready, come down slowly by bending your knees, then your hips and finally placing your feet on the ground. Keep your head down and sit back on your heels in the child's pose (see page 94) for 2–3 minutes before sitting up.

Caution: Do not attempt the headstand if you are more than four months' pregnant, menstruating or if you have high blood pressure.

Nasagra drishti – Nasal gaze

Begin your practice with nasal gazing. Sit in a comfortable meditative position with your back straight and your head erect. Gaze at the tip of your nose with your eyelids half-closed. Do this for only 10 seconds. Then close and relax your eyes. Gradually you may build up to 1 minute, as long as your eyes do not feel strained.

Bhrumadhya drishti – Frontal gaze

When you have perfected the nasal gaze, and can do it without experiencing tension, try turning your eyes upward toward the point between your eyebrows. Maintain this gaze for only 3–10 seconds. Then rest and relax your eyes. Prolonged practice of the frontal gaze is not recommended.

Other movements for ajna

Eye exercises; if your energy tends to be top-heavy, exercises with dance and music may help to distribute some of the excess to the rest of your body

Nasagra drishti –
Nasal gaze

Bhrumadhya drishti –
Frontal gaze

CHAPTER TEN

The Sahasrara Chakra

"By focusing on the light emanating from the crown of your head, you become able to see enlightened Masters."

Patanjali, *Yoga Sutra*, 3.33

INTRODUCING
Sahasrara Chakra

The sahasrara is your gateway to infinite consciousness. It is through this chakra that you are able to connect with and experience the blissful state of Absolute Knowledge that yogis call "satchidananda". This is beyond the realm of your individual awareness, which is known as the "chitta". The sahasrara provides the energetic connection by which you are able to transcend your mundane sense of duality, that is your experience of yourself and other, subject and object, masculine and feminine. It provides the metaphysical framework for your life. The sahasrara chakra is at the top end of the central meridian (sushumna nadi), where the other two major meridians (ida and pingala – ordinary consciousness) do not reach.

Healing functions
Blockages in the sahasrara chakra often leave you with a feeling of being scattered. You may lack inspiration, lead a joyless existence, see the world in a purely rational and materialistic manner and experience a sense of disconnection from all spiritual sources.

SAHASRARA BENEFITS

- Intuitive knowledge
- Deeper understanding
- Strong spiritual links
- Enhanced sense of wonder
- Discovery of divine "mysteries"
- Experience of your Higher Self
- Connection to the Divine
- Experience of completeness

LOCATION

At the top of your head (the crown), extending upward toward "heaven"

KEYWORDS

Infinite, limitless, heaven, spiritual connection, higher wisdom, enlightenment, cosmic consciousness, transcendence, immanence, union, communion, divinity, mysticism, samadhi

ASPIRATIONS

To go beyond boundaries of your individual mind and consciousness

WORKING WITH SAHASRARA

Strengthens connection with spiritual values, attitudes, ethics; it gives the courage to overcome hardship in life

ENHANCES

Your sense of wonder. Enables you to lead a life filled with joy.

The sahasrara chakra is your connection to that which is never changing, everlasting and infinite.

Using Sahasrara Chakra

Working with the energy of your crown chakra brings you intuitive knowledge, deeper understanding, strong spiritual links and an enhanced sense of wonder. It enables you to connect with other planes of existence and to discover divine "mysteries".

The crown chakra is your energetic passageway from mundane consciousness to the experience of your Higher Self. It is your connection to the Divine, to the collective unconscious and to absolute freedom. It is your gateway to immortality. Working with your crown chakra gives you the experience of completeness.

People who can access the energy of the crown chakra at will are often perceived as miracle workers. This is because they seem to be divinely guided and able to transcend the laws of nature.

Celebrate the mystical in your everyday life by taking some time to sit peacefully in meditation.

THE SAHASRARA CHAKRA

When to work with the energy of your sahasrara chakra

• You would like to establish a regular meditation practice.

• You are having trouble quieting the "chatter" in your mind.

• You suffer from insomnia or other sleep disturbances.

• You feel that you lack clear direction in life.

• You would like to receive guidance from higher realms.

• You realize that you have "gifts" that need developing.

• It is time to bring more joy and wonder into your life.

• You would like to have greater access to, and more understanding of, the workings of your unconscious and the subconscious minds.

• You become aware of the need to make changes to your basic belief system.

SAHASRARA JOURNALING — SUGGESTED QUESTIONS

• In what ways do I/could I celebrate the mystical in my everyday life?

• How could I stop being controlled by my cravings for possessions and sensual pleasure?

• What could I do to be more open to intuitive guidance?

• What would help me to see the world as a manifestation of the Divine?

• Who am I, if I am not limited by this body and this mind?

• In what ways does my desire to possess things add to my karmic burden?

• How content do I feel with what life has brought me?

Symbolic Element and Energy

Working with your crown chakra makes it possible for you to experience a state of consciousness in which you feel the unity of your human personality with your Higher Self. Your sense of isolation disappears into the understanding of the One-ness of all being.

Meaning of name: sahasra = one thousand; sahasrara = the "Lotus of the Thousand Petals"

Position: uppermost chakra, located just above the top of your head

Pattern of radiant energy: an infinite number of radiant petals, emanating lights that comprise all the colours of the rainbow. This includes all colours that are visible to the human eye, as well as the limitless number of colours that are beyond ordinary perception. In Western tradition, the sahasrara chakra is often associated with the colour violet, yet many people see it as being white, which contains all colours.

Element: beyond time and space

Geometric form representing the Infinite: there is no geometric form, only a symbolic lotus with an unlimited number of petals. In Indian tradition, the number one thousand represents the Infinite.

Mantra of element: the sound of silence; the subtle sound of all mantras and all sounds. The Buddhist mantra "OM Mani Padme Hum" (the Jewel in the Lotus) makes a strong connection with the energy of the sahasrara chakra.

Goals: enlightenment; Satchidananda (which means Absolute Truth, Absolute Consciousness and Absolute Bliss)

Age of development: adult

Consciousness: universal and spiritual awareness develops

Female energy: Yakini, who has countless faces and can see in all directions. She shines with all colours.

Positive experience: intuitive guidance, mystical awareness

Negative experience: attachment, spiritual ignorance, the void, dark night of the soul

Predominant sense: beyond the mind and all physical senses

Basic activity: meditation and the experience of joy

Sahasrara chakra presides over all aspects of the vital energy in all living beings

In Indian tradition the number one thousand is symbolic of the Infinite. Sahasrara is a "flower" of infinite energy rays.

Meditating on Sahasrara Yantra

By working with the sahasrara yantra, you may experience a deeper connection with the mystical aspects of your life. A yantra is a tool that works like a weaver's loom, but on a very subtle level. By meditating on the sahasrara yantra, you weave yourself a new, more joyous "reality".

① Place a picture of the sahasrara chakra on your meditation table, slightly below your eye level. Light a candle; if you choose to burn incense, be sure to use sandalwood.

② Sit in a comfortable meditative position and half-close your eyes.

③ Fix your gaze on the top of the picture, at "12 o'clock". Begin by looking at the blue-coloured outer gateway of the yantra. It symbolizes the east, where the sun rises.

④ Slowly rotate your eyes clockwise around the four gateways – representing the world, with its four compass points. Notice the red gate on the right, representing the south. Then look at the yellow gate at the bottom, which stands for the west. Finally look at the green gate on the left, which signifies the north.

⑤ After several rounds, allow your eyes to begin to slowly spiral inward, looking at each of the petals as though it is a step toward the golden centre. Eventually you will find yourself at the energetic centre of the yantra. Try to hold your concentration on the bindu (the dot) at the heart of the picture.

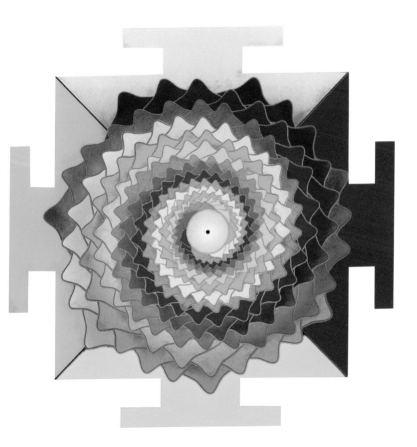

Sahasrara Imbalances

If the energy of your sahasrara is blocked or unbalanced, it is likely that you will find your mind going in one direction, your heart in another and your body in yet a third. A misaligned crown chakra may cause you to be excessively self-centred because you are unable to see the interconnectedness of life. You may be a low-energy person or your energy may circulate only in the lower chakras, directed toward totally materialistic and sensual pursuits. Your life may seem to be lacking in spiritual richness. You may not believe that anything exists beyond what can be perceived with your senses or understood with your mind. Or you may suffer from a poor perception of reality or find it difficult to "connect" in general.

In your physical body, extreme blockages may result in paralysis or multi-system diseases that affect both muscles and nerves, such as multiple sclerosis or Lou Gehrig disease (ALS). Many genetic disorders seem to be karmically linked to sahasrara blockages.

Without balancing the energy of the sahasrara chakra you will be unable to reach the superconscious state that the yogis refer to as "samadhi".

What to look for

Scepticism, extreme materialistic mentality, overindulgence in sensual pleasures – or totally denying yourself any enjoyment. You may distrust life in general or be prone to depression. You may have difficulty accepting the premises of religious and spiritual thought, humanitarianism and the concept of selflessness. Perhaps you have feelings of being scattered and lack inspiration or higher goals in life.

When your crown chakra is blocked or unbalanced, people who are sensitive to energetic values will notice that a dark, muddy colour taints your entire aura. They may experience a tingling or prickling sensation in their crown chakra when in contact with you.

Possible causes of imbalances

A variety of traumas may cause imbalances of sahasrara energy, including intense physical privation or near-death experiences. You may have been cheated, robbed of your money or abused (sexually or otherwise) by someone posing as a religious or spiritual teacher, whose actual intention was to manipulate and control you. It is even possible that you, or someone close to you, was lured into a cult and then had trouble leaving it.

WHEN SAHASRARA ENERGY IS EXCESSIVE

- You are too open to anyone who professes to be a religious or spiritual teacher.

- You may demand teachings that you are not ready to understand.

- You tend to practise excessively, but without any real understanding of the meaning of your practice.

- You may mortify your physical body with extreme practices, such as excessive fasting.

- You may have frightening visions and feel that God/angels/saints are talking only to you.

- You may feel light-headed and dizzy and perhaps suffer from frequent headaches.

WHEN SAHASRARA ENERGY IS DEFICIENT

- You tend to have a total absence of faith.

- You think that people who do have faith are either fools or hypocrites.

- You may feel isolated, alienated and disconnected from the world.

- You may be bored and apathetic.

- Without the pull toward the higher realms, your life may be stuck in the experiences of the lower chakras that deal primarily with survival and pleasure.

Balancing Sahasrara Energy

In yoga tradition, this universe is created by the original vibration of the sound of OM. Sound has three aspects: the sound you hear, its meaning and how you process it mentally. Nadanusandhana is an excellent exercise to bring all of these aspects into balance – and to connect you with the mystical meaning of OM.

Nadanusandhana – integrating the aspects of OM
Sit in any comfortable meditative position to perform this exercise.

Chant "aaa" with your mouth wide open

1 Adopt chin mudra: join the tips of your thumb and index finger on each hand. Allow your other fingers to be outstretched, but relaxed. Rest the backs of your hands on your thighs.

Chin mudra

2 Inhale slowly and completely until your lungs are full. Open your mouth wide and chant "aaa" for one full exhalation of your breath. Feel the sound resonating in your abdomen and the lower parts of your body. Repeat this nine times.

Chant "ou" with your mouth rounded

1 Adopt chinmaya mudra: join the tips of the thumb and index finger on each hand. Then fold your middle, ring and little fingers in to touch the palms. Rest the backs of your hands on your thighs.

Chinmaya mudra

② Inhale slowly and completely until your lungs are full. Round your lips and chant "ou" for one full exhalation of your breath. Feel the sound resonating in your chest and the middle part of your body. Repeat this nine times.

Chant "mmm" with your lips sealed

① Adopt adi mudra: fold each of your thumbs in to touch the palm of the same hand. Then fold the other fingers over it. Rest the backs of your hands on your thighs.

Adi mudra

② Inhale slowly and completely until your lungs are full. Keep your mouth closed and chant "mmm" for one full exhalation of your breath. Feel the sound resonating in your head region. Repeat this nine times.

Chant A-U-M starting with your mouth wide open and finishing with your lips sealed

① Adopt brahma mudra; this is similar to adi mudra, but place your fists on either side of your navel.

② Inhale slowly and completely until your lungs are full. Chant "aa" with your mouth wide open, gradually rounding your lips to chant "ou" and continuing to round your lips until your mouth is closed and you are chanting "mmm". Feel the sound resonating throughout your body. Repeat this nine times.

Brahma mudra

Sahasrara Relationships

Your crown chakra may be compared to an antenna that sends and receives energetic information relating specifically to spiritual values and mystical relationships. Most connections here would tend to be non-secular and non-physical in nature.

If you are a spiritual aspirant, sahasrara energy is how you connect with your mentor when receiving teachings. It enables you to commune with God or feel at one with nature. The crown chakra is where you would establish connections to beings in other realms or vibratory levels, such as spirit guides, angels or ascended masters.

Communication through the chakras

In a positive relationship, teachings pass from teacher to student on an intellectual (ajna) as well as intuitive (sahasrara) level. But the student is not expected to accept things blindly. There is open communication at the vishuddha chakra; the student feels free to ask questions. The teacher unreservedly gives answers and does not hesitate to question the student about his or her practice.

There is also energetic exchange at the heart chakra. The teacher and student each feel a deep (non-physical) love and compassion for each other. The teacher may empathize with the student's difficulties and offer advice. The student accepts this, as he or she trusts the teacher and understands that there is no hidden agenda.

In the diagram of an unhealthy teacher–student relationship (opposite), the teacher has so overwhelmed the student intellectually, verbally and through his or her charisma that the student does not notice there is actually no connection at the sahasrara. Instead, he or she has submitted to a sexual relationship (swadhisthana) – and the unselfish love (anahata) is one-way. In using the student the teacher is abusing the relationship.

A HEALTHY SPIRITUAL TEACHER–STUDENT RELATIONSHIP

spiritual teacher   **student**

Energy exchange at sahasrara (crown) chakra

Intellectual (ajna) energy passed to student

Communication at vishuddha (throat) chakra

Non-physical love and compassion exchanged at anahata (heart) chakra

AN UNHEALTHY TEACHER–STUDENT RELATIONSHIP

teacher   **student**

No connection at sahasrara (crown) chakra

Student overwhelmed intellectually (ajna)

Student overwhelmed verbally (vishuddha)

One-way communication at anahata (heart) chakra

Student overwhelmed with manipura energy (teacher's charisma)

Sexual connection at swadhisthana (sacral) chakra

Sahasrara Meditation

Meditation on your sahasrara chakra gives you a feeling of liberation, completeness and spiritual connection. This experience is expressed as fullness (poorna) or the Absolute (Brahman) by yogis. It is the vision of the void (shunya) that is described in Buddhist philosophy.

Meditation on Divine Light

1 Sit in your chosen meditation position, making sure that your spine is straight. Bring your hands together in your lap with the palms upward; have your left hand on top. This is the mudra of receiving energy. Close your eyes; make your breathing slow and even. Focus your attention on the crown of your head.

2 Visualize a bright white light flowing in through your crown chakra. Feel Divine Light spiralling down through your body. Enjoy the warm glow of the Light as it saturates your entire being. Every cell of your physical body is being permeated by Light and Divine Inspiration. All levels of your mind and consciousness are illumined by Divine Light.

3 You may choose to repeat the following affirmations, or create similar ones that are more meaningful to you:

• I am surrounded and protected by Divine Light.

• This Light sustains and nourishes my entire being.

• I am ever walking in the Light.

• I feel myself growing stronger as I tune in to the Light.

4 Sit silently for at least 15–20 minutes, allowing yourself to be at one with the Light. The Divine Light is a manifestation of your Higher Self. It is a representation of the peace that is beyond all rational understanding. Feel that you are a pure channel for the Light. In this state of Oneness, intuitive thoughts and inspirations may enter your consciousness. Be thankful for this guidance.

⑤ You may also choose to think of someone you know who is in need of Divine Light. Repeat the exercise by visualizing that person as being bathed in Light. The Light is entering through the top of his/her head and spiralling downward, just as it did into your body. Repeat the affirmations, using the person's name:

- [Insert name] is surrounded and protected by Divine Light.

- This Light sustains and nourishes [insert name]'s entire being.

- [Insert name] is ever walking in the Light.

- May [insert name] ever grow strong by tuning in to the Light.

⑥ Before you stand up, give thanks that you are able to share the Light. Then take a few deep breaths before you open your eyes.

In the meditation on Divine Light, you feel as though a blissful radiance is illuminating your entire being.

Working with Sahasrara

Your crown chakra is the seat of transcendent pure consciousness that is beyond the realm of your ordinary individual awareness. Its energy makes it possible to experience a superconscious state that is beyond time and space. You become fully aware of the identification of your individual personality with the higher Self.

High namaskar

① Stand erect with your feet 2–4in (5–10cm) apart. Make sure that your weight is evenly distributed. Inhale deeply and, as you exhale, bring your palms together at your chest in the namaskar position. Hold this pose for a few moments, being particularly aware of your feet grounding your body.

② Then slowly straighten your elbows and stretch your arms upward. Hold the position for 1–3 minutes, feeling your energy elongating upward.

③ Bringing your hands down, separate your feet, bend your knees slightly and drop your head down between your legs to relax. Visualize the energy of the crown of your head connecting with the earth.

Ardha-chandrasana – Half moon pose

① Stand erect with your feet 2–4in (5–10cm) apart. Make sure that your weight is evenly distributed. Inhale as you stretch your arms straight out to the sides and then over your head in a lateral, circular motion. When your hands meet, interlock your fingers.

② Release your index fingers so that they are pointing upward. Keep your elbows straight and try to bring your arms behind your ears as much as possible. Stretch your entire body upward, keeping your chin parallel to the ground and away from your chest.

High namaskar

Ardha-chandrasana –
Half moon pose

Look straight ahead as you exhale and bend toward the right. Bring your top hip and shoulder back as much as possible; do not allow your body to twist. Check yourself to make sure that your weight is still distributed equally and that your chin is away from your chest.

 Inhale as you return to centre. Repeat on the other side.

Vrischikasana – Scorpion pose

The scorpion is an advanced pose requiring intensive mental focus and upper back flexibility. Be sure that you have perfected the headstand, and can hold it comfortably for at least 3 minutes, before attempting the scorpion.

① Get into the headstand (see page 206).

② Bend your knees and arch backward, making sure that your weight remains on your elbows. Release the interlock of your fingers and bring your hands flat on the ground. Try to keep your forearms as parallel as possible.

③ Lift your head and try to bring your shoulders directly over your elbows. Look up, as much as possible. Hold the position for as long as you feel comfortable. To maintain this, you must be fully present in the moment. It enables you to become more aware of yourself as the one who is witnessing the world.

Caution: Do not attempt the scorpion if you are menstruating, pregnant or suffer from neck injuries.

Other activities for sahasrara

Meditation

Vrischikasana –
Scorpion pose

CHAPTER ELEVEN

Chakra Inter-relationships

In reality, the actions and characteristics of the various chakras can only be separated intellectually. This chapter explores how the chakras interconnect with each other. To understand each chakra, it is important to see the bigger picture: no chakra works in isolation.

Muladhara Chakra

Your muladhara chakra is your energetic foundation. When it is firm, you not only feel more secure in life in general, but you also have a firm basis from which you can work with your other chakras.

Muladhara–swadhisthana

Taken together, the two lowest chakras work jointly to govern your instincts. This includes your personal survival as well as your sexuality and your ability to adapt to a situation.

Muladhara–manipura

When the energy of your first and third chakras is balanced, you feel grounded and able to "stand on your own two feet". Your self-image, will-power and sense of personal power (usually seen as the realm of the manipura chakra) are all strongly affected by muladhara energy, as well as how secure you feel, especially in relation to such issues as wealth, nourishment and family and other relationships.

Muladhara–anahata

How generous you are by nature often depends on how vulnerable you feel in life. An imbalance in the lowest chakra might cause you to cling to, and crave, more possessions because you never feel as though you have enough: insecurity often leads to stockpiling energy and possessions. It may also involve a tightening of your heart when you are asked to share what you have with others.

Muladhara–vishuddha

Basic insecurity (imbalance in muladhara energy) can often lead to hoarding and over-consumption. When the energetic flow between your base (muladhara) and throat (vishuddha) chakras is blocked or distorted, the vishuddha can become the seat of your addictions.

Many negative habits and cravings have obvious connections with the throat: alcoholism, smoking, gossiping, overeating. Other obsessions may stem from your inability to feel safe and satisfied. Energetic imbalances in the throat (vishuddha) chakra often play an important role in people becoming shopaholics or developing eating disorders such as anorexia, bulimia, excessive dieting and bingeing.

Muladhara–ajna
The energy of the muladhara chakra provides the solid support for your mental discipline. It supports your intellectual development.

Muladhara–sahasrara
The energy of the muladhara chakra also provides the feelings of security that are essential for your spiritual practice and cosmic connection. The balance between the crown (sahasrara) and base (muladhara) chakras determines how fully you are able to inhabit and enjoy being in your physical body. And, from the position of being rooted in your body, this connection enables you to choose the type of spiritual practice in which to engage.

Balancing and grounding yourself through the energy of muladhara chakra can help you to explore such questions as: "How do I ground myself without getting stuck?"

Swadhisthana Chakra

Balancing the energy of the swadhisthana chakra with that of your other chakras can enhance the benefits of working with the other chakras. It helps to strengthen your immune system (muladhara), gives you more vitality (manipura), enhances your sensitivity and empathy (anahata), stimulates your artistic ability (vishuddha), enables you to cultivate greater intellectual prowess (ajna) – as well as making you more attractive. All aspects of your body and mind become fluid and adaptable. When the energy of your sacral (swadhisthana) chakra is functioning well, you don't need to always win, control, get even and/or impress others.

Contrary to popular belief, working with the swadhisthana (sacral) chakra is not about enhancing your sexuality. For the swadhisthana to be fully functional and balanced, the sex drive must be sublimated into a force of awareness – it must be balanced with the energies of your other chakras, which can help you to gain new insights into relationships with friends, family and colleagues at work.

Swadhisthana–muladhara

Muladhara is "stability" while swadhisthana is "flow". Adaptability is important; it helps you to release the past, empowers you to drop those things that might be hindering your growth and enables you to accept transitions. This may involve letting go of what is familiar, safe and secure (muladhara energy) and travelling to (as yet) unknown places of the soul.

However, if your swadhisthana energy overpowers that of muladhara, your life might flow too much: you may be in a constant state of flux, unable to ground yourself. In order for you to be secure and grounded, but not to feel stuck in your life, you need to get right the balance between these two energies.

Swadhisthana–manipura

Vanity, guilt and embarrassment or shame about your body are powerful negative sentiments that are usually associated with blockages in your swadhisthana chakra. When these feelings are habitual, they can greatly undermine your self-esteem (manipura).

Alternatively, poor self-image can result in a need for you to constantly send out sexual messages. The ability to discern when it is appropriate to open or close your second chakra is an important one. You may want to open up emotionally when you are with friends or family members, and sexually with your partner, yet you may not want to have the same openness when you walk down a crowded street or when you are at work. The issue of opening chakras will be dealt with more fully in the next chapter (see page 260).

If you do not deal adequately with the negative emotions of fear and shame from the lower two chakras, they can distort the energy of your solar plexus (manipura) chakra by overstimulating it, thus producing anger.

Swadhisthana–anahata

These two chakras, working in unison, determine how selfish or unselfish your relationships are. This balance is especially important with regard to the various aspects of love. Together, the sacral (swadhisthana) and heart (anahata) chakras control the

love and sexuality issues in your relationships. For example, "love at first sight" may involve sexual attraction, which develops to combine with an empathic relationship.

Amplifying the energy of your swadhisthana chakra, without also balancing and purifying the energy of your heart (anahata) chakra, can lead to an unhealthy exaggeration of your sexuality. When this happens, you will probably find that your relationships are more temporary and their scope is more limited.

Swadhisthana–vishuddha

The energies of these two chakras are very strongly linked, as they represent two essential aspects of creativity. See page 244 for an understanding of the special relationship that exists between the swadhisthana and vishuddha chakras.

If your sacral (swadhisthana) and throat (vishuddha) chakras are not in balance, you may find that your voice is either too deep or too shrill.

Swadhisthana–ajna

Although the manipura chakra is said to govern your sense of sight, there are many ways of seeing, other than the physical. For example, when a mother does not "see" her husband sexually abusing their daughter, this represents a breakdown of communication between manipura (physical sight), ajna (consciously being aware of) and swadhisthana (sexuality) chakras.

Dreams are in the watery domain of swadhisthana, but they express the contents of your mind (ajna). If you allow yourself to spend too much time dreaming or attach too much importance to sense gratification, the energy of the sacral (swadhisthana) chakra may go out of balance. In Indian tradition, the fish who allows himself to be caught because of his greed (over-attachment to sense of taste) is symbolic of an imbalance between the swadhisthana and ajna chakras.

Swadhisthana–sahasrara

Blockages in your crown (sahasrara) chakra may cause you to deny yourself, and even fear, the most minimal pleasures. This represents an imbalance between the swadhisthana and sahasrara chakras, and is very different from the principle of simple living undertaken as a spiritual practice.

Meditation to strengthen the sacral–heart connection

Variations of this meditation may be used to strengthen the connection between any of your chakras.

① Sit in a comfortable meditative position with your back straight. Breathe gently through your nostrils.

② Feel as though your breath is making an energetic circuit between your sacral (swadhisthana) and heart chakras. As you inhale feel as though you are drawing prana in through your heart centre (anahata) and that prana is moving in a circular motion to your sacral region.

③ As you exhale, feel the energy moving upward and returning to the heart.

CONNECTING SWADHISTHANA AND ANAHATA

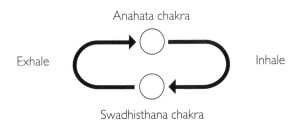

Anahata chakra

Exhale

Inhale

Swadhisthana chakra

Manipura Chakra

Whether you are seeking to transform energy into material form or thought into action, the manipura and ajna chakras need to be working in harmony with each other. They have a special relationship. Your solar plexus chakra (manipura) is like a battery, or primary energy source, that energizes all of the other the chakras – including the ajna chakra.

In some Eastern martial arts traditions, the manipura chakra is known as the "hara" point. It is the physical centre of your body and governs homeostasis, balance and equilibrium in the body itself. Yet, to be most effective, it must work in harmony with the ajna chakra, which is the seat of a balanced mind.

Physical sight is governed by the radiant energy of manipura, but it is the ajna chakra that determines how you "see" the world and yourself. It is the energy of ajna (often referred to as the "third eye" or "mind's eye") that allows you to see intuitively, opening you up to psychic perceptions and allowing you to see the "bigger picture".

Manipura enables you to see and explore the world; ajna enables you to understand what you see, including the importance of a healthy give and take of energy on your voyage through life. With the development of the ajna chakra, you begin to acquire insight into the meaning, deeper dimensions and goals of your life.

Manipura is where gut feelings arise. Successful entrepreneurs, astute business people, winning gamblers and shrewd criminals are all experts at being able to harness these feelings to their advantage. But to convert these feelings into a successful plan of action, the energy of ajna, the seat of disciplined thought, must be accessed.

MANIPURA	AJNA
Physical sight	Intuition; insight; vision of your higher purpose in life; clairvoyance
Physical hunger and digestion	Intellectual and spiritual yearning; assimilation of ideas and experiences
Physical energy; the vigour to put your intellectual understandings into action; will-power	Intellectual understanding and rational thought
Balanced body and steady movements	Balanced attitude toward life. Determination of the direction in which you intend to take your body. Ajna is where you make the decisions as to where you want your body's movements to take you.
Will-power; the strength and determination to carry out the decisions you make	Decision-making principle

Manipura–vishuddha–swadhisthana

Your solar plexus (manipura) also has a special relationship with your throat (vishuddha) and sacral (swadhisthana) chakras. Together they govern your actions and attitudes toward food and eating issues, digestion and consumption. Swadhisthana relates to your sense of taste, yet the actual actions of eating and tasting are controlled by your throat (vishuddha) chakra. The digestion of food is governed by manipura.

Anahata Chakra

Increasing the activity of your physical heart does not necessarily assist in releasing blockages in the energy flow of your anahata chakra. It may actually depress the chakra's efficient functioning if you direct your energy solely toward physical matter, rather than aiming at the enhancement of your inner consciousness.

When the energy of your heart chakra is flowing in a healthy, unblocked manner, negative emotions are swept away by the "winds" of change. Fear, guilt, shame and anger, the negative emotions of the lower chakras, evaporate when you have a "change of heart".

Your heart chakra (anahata) is the body's energetic centre. A major part of its job is to keep the other chakras in balance.

Anahata–muladhara

When the heart (anahata) and base (muladhara) chakras are working together in harmony, your compassion is more than an airy feeling; it is grounded and purposeful.

Anahata–swadhisthana

If there is a blockage between the heart (anahata) and sacral (swadhisthana) chakras, you may tend to look to others to fulfil your emotional needs. Or, you may confuse love with sexual attraction.

Anahata–manipura

An energetic "bridge" develops between your manipura and anahata chakras when you begin to realize that just collecting more material "stuff" is not enough to make you happy. Up until this point you have been basing your identity on your possessions.

The connection between the two chakras really becomes functional with your first authentic act of forgiveness. Your energetic awakening can proceed no further without forgiveness. To strengthen this connection, ask yourself:

"Who must I forgive in order to be free?"

"What do I need to forgive myself for?"

Anahata–vishuddha

Unblocking your throat (vishuddha) chakra usually involves deep listening to your own heart, tuning in to silence, becoming a good listener and developing empathy. Normal communication is from vishuddha, but a "heart-to-heart" connection involves anahata as well. Whereas silence can be golden, if you command your children to "be quiet" too often, you may be doing more than hampering their ability to interact with the world. You may also be contributing to the creation of a major blockage in their chakras. For healthy communication to take place, the energy of the heart (anahata), throat (vishuddha) and brow (ajna) chakras need to be unblocked and communicating with each other.

Anahata–ajna

This is one of the most important chakra connections. When a thought comes into your mind, if the connection between your mind and your heart is blocked, even partially, your ideas, hopes and dreams cannot be realized.

Anahata–sahasrara

Your heart connects your humanity with your divinity. When there is a strong working relationship between these two chakras, all forms of love tend to take on higher spiritual dimensions.

SPECIAL RELATIONSHIP WITH SWADHISTHANA
Vishuddha Chakra

Creative impulses are an integral aspect of your swadhisthana chakra; they can be expressed in a variety of ways. You can create physically using the energy of the sacral chakra (swadhisthana) itself or you can communicate your impulses to others and express yourself in language or artistically, using the energy of your throat chakra (vishuddha) in conjunction with that of swadhisthana.

When your swadhisthana and vishuddha chakras are open, balanced and fully working together, you blossom as a sensitive, intuitive, idealistic and artistic person, who is full of dreams and able to express them. You are adaptable and able to accept change as an aspect of your life. You don't wallow in emotional self-pity, nor are you in the habit of complaining excessively when things go wrong in your life. The energy of your sacral chakra (swadhisthana) supports that of your throat chakra (vishuddha) in finding your own truth and expressing it in your own terms. A free flow of energy between these two chakras brings you freedom from emotional neediness; it satisfies your thirst for self-expression.

Your need to be "heard" becomes increasingly difficult to meet if either of these two chakras goes out of balance and your creativity does not flow properly. You may find yourself experiencing a situation akin to "writer's block". If the communication between chakras is blocked, even partially, you will tend to feel it both emotionally and physically. When this happens, it seems that nothing in life is good enough; nothing seems to make you happy.

An inability to express yourself in language or otherwise can result in your having a lack of enduring personal relationships, a reliance on comfort eating as a substitute for authentic emotional gratification, and extreme stress. To restore balance, you may find a guided healing or 12-step programme helpful.

VISHUDDHA	SWADHISTHANA
Artistic creativity, aural creation, command of speech; ability to compose poetry, understand dreams, be a good teacher (especially a spiritual teacher)	Physical creativity
Inspiration to begin a project and see it to completion	Giving birth to a child; physical energy to give birth to a project
Taste is experienced physically by your throat	The ability to "taste" the sweetness of all that life has to offer
Self-expression	Self-gratification
Blockages are often the result of verbal abuse (especially experienced as a child), excessive criticism, being forced to keep secrets, blackmail (especially emotional), lies and mixed messages.	Blockages are often the result of emotional and sexual abuse, such as incest, rape, abortion. Perhaps you were neglected, either physically or emotionally, as a child and experienced a sense of rejection and/or emotional manipulation.
You might have been brought up in an authoritarian way, constantly admonished with "Don't talk back".	Perhaps you come from a staunch religious family with a moral aversion to pleasure.
Perhaps your family has a history of alcoholism and family members tend to shout instead of talking to each other.	Your family might have a history of alcoholism – or may be one in which physical and psychological abuse was accepted as the norm. You may have been forced to take on an adult role too early, with responsibilities that you were not yet equipped to handle.
Energy of language	Energy of emotion

Ajna Chakra

Commonly known as your "third eye" or the "mind's eye", the ajna chakra is the command centre of your subtle body. It is your inner instrument, whose job it is to manage your five senses (sight, hearing, smell, taste and touch) plus your mind. It also regulates all of your other chakras and the nadis (energy channels) leading into them.

Your brow centre (ajna) may become depleted and cut off from the other chakras if you are in the habit of allowing the energy of your lower chakras to be wasted. A balanced ajna chakra requires stable lower chakras to support it.

Alternatively, a healthy ajna chakra tends to encourage balance in the lower chakras. For this reason, many yogis suggest that it is best to begin your chakra work with your ajna chakra. The brow centre tends to be the easiest to rouse – and often stimulates the other chakras to open simultaneously. Once the energy of your ajna chakra is balanced, it helps to counteract any negative effects that may occur in your other chakras.

Ajna–m ara

When these two chakras are working well together, you have a healthy balance of instinct and logic. It is important, when you begin doing inner work, not to let yourself become ungrounded. As you become increasingly aware of your spiritual dimensions, do not lose touch with your physical needs. Purifying and balancing muladhara energy with that of ajna will enable you to function in the present moment. It will also aid you in bringing your intellectual ideals to full fruition.

Ajna–swadhisthana

Your sacral chakra is more concerned with your gratification. Its power lies in actuating immediate self-fulfilment, as opposed to logically working things out, which is why it is important for swadhisthana to work with the ajna chakra.

Anja–manipura
Your raw gut feelings (manipura) are honed into intuition (ajna) by these two chakras working in unison. Healthy communication between your brow centre (ajna) and your solar plexus (manipura) encourages mental balance and equilibrium.

Ajna–anahata
Compassion, love, forgiveness, trust, hope and emotional self-empowerment are impulses that arise from your heart. If they are not thought through properly, you may act impulsively or irrationally. It is important to ensure that your "head" and "heart" are always in agreement and working with each other.

Ajna–vishuddha
The connection of the brow (ajna) and throat (vishuddha) chakras remains fully functional when you think before speaking.

Ajna–sahasrara
The brow (ajna) and crown (sahasrara) chakras often work together to transmute the experiences of your multi-dimensional inner universe into a comprehensible form.

Sahasrara Chakra

The highest of the seven major chakras, the sahasrara may also be seen as more than a chakra; it is your connection to the energy of the universe itself. When the crown chakra (sahasrara) is blocked you are less receptive to energy, so less prana is transmitted to the other chakras.

Sahasrara–muladhara

The grounding of your base chakra (muladhara) provides the foundation for the healthy functioning of your sahasrara. This relationship is the basis for your spiritual practice and enlightenment.

With your concerted effort, the potential energy that is lying dormant at your muladhara (base) chakra can be brought to full manifestation at the crown chakra (sahasrara). Indian mythology gives the image of the serpent power, known as "kundalini", who transmutes herself into the thousand-headed serpent known as "sesha" as she travels up through the various stages of awareness. At the root chakra (muladhara), kundalini represents unlimited potential energy. When this energy is awakened and brought up through your various chakras until it reaches your crown chakra (sahasrara), your illusion of being separate from the rest of the universe is dissolved.

When the energy of your crown chakra (sahasrara) is unbalanced, you may become so preoccupied with spiritual matters that you disregard the basic human needs for food, shelter, survival and even love. It is as though you are no longer fully living on the earth. But this does not necessarily mean that you are more spiritual or "closer to God".

This type of obsessive behaviour actually indicates an unhealthy imbalance between the energies of the sahasrara and muladhara, chakras, the two chakras that define the polarities of your being.

Neither one is more important than the other; their energies need to be in balance for you to lead a healthy and happy existence that includes a deep spiritual element.

Sahasrara–swadhisthana

When the energy of your crown chakra (sahasrara) is unbalanced, you may fail to connect with the ongoing flow of life. You may deny yourself even the simplest of pleasures. For a peaceful, balanced existence, sahasrara must have an amicable working relationship with swadhisthana.

Sahasrara–manipura

Your solar plexus reflects your concept of personal freedom; sahasrara is concerned with your freedom from the illusion of being disconnected from the oneness of nature.

Sahasrara–anahata

When your energy is flowing freely between the crown (sahasrara) and heart (anahata) chakras, you are able to "give" of yourself wholeheartedly. You feel inspired to contribute to the greater good, as well as receive from the universal source. In general, you have a healthy connection with the bigger picture in life and experience a kinship with all beings.

Sahasrara–vishuddha

When communication between the crown (sahasrara) and throat (vishuddha) chakras is blocked or distorted, you tend to understand spiritual teachings literally rather than connecting with their true spirit. You may be fanatical and dogmatic.

Sahasrara–ajna

The two highest chakras have a special working relationship, whose goal is your total freedom and inner peace.

MEDITATION

Meditation on the Inter-relationship of the Elements

In this meditation you use your mind to connect the energies of your various chakras. You begin with your physical body, which is composed of the five elements; each one of those elements is governed by a specific chakra.

First, you think of how your body will become cold at the time of your death as the fire element leaves it. Your body will bloat up as the gases leave it; dry up as the water leave it; and the earth element will return to the earth as your body decomposes. Finally your body will cease to occupy space as it disintegrates completely.

Then, you visualize how each of the physical elements, starting with earth, the most dense, is merged with the element that is more subtle. The earth element of your root chakra (muladhara) is merged with water. The water element of the sacral chakra (swadhisthana) is merged with fire. The fire element of the solar plexus chakra (manipura) is merged with air. The air element of the heart chakra (anahata) is merged with ether. The ether of your throat chakra (vishuddha) is merged with your mind at the brow chakra (ajna). Finally, your mind is merged with the absolute consciousness of the crown chakra (sahasrara).

This is the reverse of the process by which the earth was formed. Before our planet became solid it was liquid, like the molten lava of a volcano. Before it was liquid it was "fire", like the sun, and before this fire there was only a mass of swirling gasses (air). Before these gases came into being, they existed as primordial space – which came from the Supreme Mind – which came from pure consciousness.

An ancient Indian representation of the chakra system that includes some of the minor chakras.

Meditation on the inter-relationship of the elements

You do not need to go through this entire process in your first sitting. Take some time; this exercise may take a week, or several weeks, or even several months, to complete. Sit for at least 20–30 minutes daily. With repeated practice, you will begin to experience the interconnectedness of all life. The energy of your chakras will become balanced and better able to work together harmoniously.

Sit in a comfortable meditative position with your back straight and your eyes closed. Breathe gently through your nostrils. Mentally repeat to yourself:

1 "I am not the solid matter of the base chakra (muladhara); solid matter does not define who I am in essence. Earth dissolves in water as my energy rises to my sacral chakra (swadhisthana)." Stay with this thought for some time before proceeding to the next one.

2 "Neither am I liquid matter; water does not define my essential being. Water evaporates in fire as I feel my energy ascending to the solar plexus chakra (manipura)." Stay with this thought for some time before proceeding to the next one.

3 "I am not the element of fire. Although I need heat and radiance in my life; the element of fire does not define me. Fire merges into air as my prana rises to my heart chakra (anahata)." Stay with this thought for some time before proceeding to the next one.

4 "I am not this gaseous matter; the air element of my heart chakra (anahata) does not fully delineate who I am. Air disperses in space at my throat chakra (vishuddha)." Stay with this thought for some time before proceeding to the next one.

5 "I am not the element of ether. Ether is a product of the mind. I see space being absorbed back into my mind." Stay with this thought for some time before proceeding to the next one.

6 "Instead of identifying with the limited consciousness of my individual mind, I strive to identify with the cosmos itself. My mind is derived from the universal consciousness. I see it being absorbed back into the universal consciousness at the crown chakra (sahasrara)."

To experience the inter-relatedness of chakras, hold one hand in front of one chakra and the other hand near the region of the other chakra. Close your eyes and feel as though your breath is making a circuit between the two. This is an extension of the exercise that you did to connect the anahata and swadhisthana chakras (see page 239).

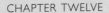

CHAPTER TWELVE

Protection During Energetic Work

"By directing your full attention to the inner
Light, you can see what is subtle, hidden from
view or at a great distance."

Patanjali, *Yoga Sutra*, 3.25

Why Protection is Needed

If you are a person who usually tends to be psychically open, you probably experience the world as a very noisy, often confusing, place. To be able to focus your energies, it is important for you to cultivate the ability to choose when to have your chakras open – and when you need some energetic protection.

If your chakras were constantly open, this would probably make you overly sensitive. You would find that your energy is constantly being drained, leaving you in a state of perpetual exhaustion. When you are in safe place, relaxing with friends or family, or when you are preparing to meditate, it is good to let your chakras open and allow your aura to expand outward. However you will probably want to pull your aura in tightly around you when you are in crowded or negative places.

Closing your chakras is quite different from blocking their energy flow. Each chakra is a mass of energy that involves a constant movement of your prana. As we have seen throughout this book, any blockage can cause severe physical, emotional, psychological and energetic problems.

Protecting yourself is rather like closing the windows of your house on a cold day. You can still see and enjoy the sun shining, but you are protected from the cold and from the street noise; you are not wasting precious heat (energy) and you can still open the door to people, should you choose. Closing your chakras is like shielding them from needless energy drain and negative input.

Preliminary steps

The first recommendations for preserving your subtle energy and protecting yourself are very simple. You need to maintain a healthy lifestyle by making sure that you get enough rest and that you eat a balanced and nutritious diet. Eating just raw foods or only brown rice can unbalance your energies and weaken your resolve. Also, exercise regularly, but do not overdo it.

Notice how the company of some people tends to drain you and start avoiding "psychic vampires" whenever possible. This may not be an option if you work in a shop or an office, where you have to deal with other people and the general public. Learn to protect yourself from being too open at the wrong times.

The world can be a noisy and confusing place if you do not have the skills and knowledge to protect yourself energetically.

How to Protect Yourself

Protection is an important part of chakra work. In every interaction you have with other people an energy exchange takes place. It is therefore important that you don't allow other people's negative energies to take over your personal space. There are many techniques that you can use to protect your chakras and your aura, which is the bio-magnetic energy that surrounds you and every other living being and extends about 2–3ft (1m) from your physical body. Here is a selection:

- Every morning, before you go out, imagine an egg-shaped bubble protecting your physical body.

- Think of a beautiful golden bubble of light surrounding you. This light will help to seal your aura.

- Imagine that you are wearing body armour made of golden light.

- If someone seems particularly insistent on draining your energy, fold your arms in front of your solar plexus.

- When you are in a crowd, bring the top of your tongue up flat against the roof of your mouth. Many martial art practitioners use this technique as energetic protection against their adversaries. It is also used by massage therapists to avoid picking up negative energies from their clients and help to prevent their energies from being drained.

SUITABLE CLOTHING

It is best not to wear ordinary clothes for meditation or chakra work, as they trap vibrations. Protect yourself by wearing loose, comfortable clothes, preferably natural fibres. Jeans are not appropriate (even if loose), as the sturdy fabric obstructs prana flow. A meditation shawl helps to contain your energy and insulate you from outside influences.

Using sound to seal each chakra

(1) Sit comfortably, with your back straight. Do the grounding exercise on page 266 and leave your "roots" deep in the earth.

(2) Bring one hand, with your palm facing toward your body, about 2in (5cm) in front of your abdomen, just below your navel. Take a deep breath and, as you exhale, chant the sound "mmm", with your lips gently closed. Feel as though the sound is resonating in, and sealing the energy of, your swadhisthana chakra.

(3) Move your hand up in front of your solar plexus and chant "mmm"; feel the sound resonating in your manipura chakra.

(4) Slide your hand up so that your palm is facing your heart centre. Breathe deeply and chant "mmm"; feel the sound resonating in your anahata chakra.

(5) Bring your hand in front of your throat. Chant "mmm" as you exhale and feel the sound vibrating in your vishuddha chakra.

(6) Bring your hand in front of your forehead and chant "mmm"; feel the sound resonating in your sinuses and ajna chakra.

(7) Raise your hand over your head, so that your palm is facing downward. Do not touch your head, but allow your hand to be suspended over it. Chant "mmm"; feel the sound resonating at your crown chakra.

You could wear a shawl or light blanket around your head and upper body to protect and insulate you during meditation.

Opening and Closing Your Chakras

Being in nature, especially near the sea or an open stretch of water, opens your chakras, as does being with those whom you love or feel connected with. Chakras also become more expansive during yoga practice, healing work and meditation.

Although it is important to be open and loving with your friends and family, it is not good to always be energetically open – or to be too absorbent. When you are overly absorbent, you allow yourself to be a receptor for any and every type of energy, including negativity. This can happen whenever you are in a public place, but especially when you are feeling "spaced out".

Practise the following exercise to gain control of the ability to open and close your chakras at will.

Expanding and contracting your chakras

It is best to do this exercise in a quiet, safe place. Try to practise at a time when you will not be disturbed. Sit in a comfortable meditation position and keep your eyes closed throughout this exercise. If you have difficulty experiencing the locations of your chakras, begin with the exercise on pages 68–9. Once you have made yourself familiar with each of the chakras, bring your awareness to the space above your head.

❶ Take a few deep breaths and then let your breath find its natural rhythm. Picture a lotus or a rose (or any other flower) that is closed. Watch intently as your flower slowly begins to open. Notice how each petal reaches out, creating a spiral pattern. Permit yourself to be overwhelmed by its beauty, fragrance and colour. See the arrangement of its petals, noticing how they spiral out from the centre of the flower.

2 Next, bring your awareness to the centre of your forehead. Visualize your unopened flower there and watch it open.

3 Repeat this process at your throat and then at your heart. As the flower opens, feel your heart opening with it. Notice how the healing warmth, radiating out from your heart centre, is creating a feeling of general well-being in every part of your body.

4 Continue moving down your body, scanning your chakra system and visualizing each chakra, in turn, opening in this way.

5 When you wish to open a chakra, visualize it as a flower unfolding slowly, with its petals opening outward, as flowers do in the morning sun. When you wish to close your chakras, start from the bottom and work up. Imagine each chakra-flower closing into a tight bud, as flowers do when the sun goes down. With regular practice, you will probably become able to open and close your chakras at will.

Before doing any yoga, meditation or spiritual work, visualize your chakras as flowers opening to the sun.

Variation using breath: Inhale as you open each chakra. Exhale sharply as you close it. The *Siva-Svarodaya*, an ancient Sanskrit text, advises that you inhale deeply as you walk toward friends and those who love and want to help you, thus opening your chakras. It then suggests that you exhale deeply as you walk toward people whom you would rather avoid, thus protecting yourself by closing your chakras.

Closing your chakras at the end of meditation

It is a good idea to consciously close your chakras the end of every meditation, yoga or healing session. This is true whether you are the teacher or student, also if you are the therapist or the person who has just had the treatment.

1. Begin by taking two or three exaggerated deep breaths and then open your eyes and look around. Do not stand up too quickly. Gradually become aware of your physical body; be attentive to the room you are in. This simple action will draw in your aura a little and start to desensitize your chakras.

2. Focus on each chakra in turn, starting with the sahasrara. Visualize it as getting smaller and more contained.

3. Then scan down your body and repeat this with each of the other chakras. With practice, this should take you no more than two minutes to complete. Be particularly aware of your manipura chakra; reinforce the closing by exhaling sharply and drawing your diaphragm upward. Yoga practitioners will recognize this movement as uddiyana bandha. It is particularly important to protect your solar plexus, as this is the main way that you make casual energetic exchanges with others. Then close the swadhisthana chakra. You may choose to leave the muladhara chakra open so that you can remain as grounded as possible.

When you have finished your practice, visualize your chakras as flowers closing in the evening.

Grounding

Grounding relates to the energy of your base chakra (muladhara) and your ability to fully inhabit your physical body. This ability, to consciously live on this earth and draw your sustenance from it, is essential for your general good health, as well as your emotional and mental well-being. Whenever you are doing any kind of work with chakras, it is best to begin by grounding yourself.

Living in an ungrounded state means that, for some reason, you have numbed yourself to emotional and physical sensations. Although this enables you to experience less pain, it also means that you may think less clearly, have difficulty in relating to the "real" world and have problems in making decisions. If taken to an extreme, you may lose touch with reality, forget to eat, have problems being on time, be hypersensitive, not listen to what is being said to you and have difficulty in reading and following instructions. In ayurveda, being ungrounded is referred to as having an excess of "vata", or wind.

If you have spent most of your life being ungrounded, grounding yourself may make you feel a bit heavy at first. However, it is well worth persevering. When your body is properly grounded you are less likely to absorb negative energy, you tend to feel less tired and you are able to go about your life with full concentration.

Carry out the grounding visualization on page 266 twice daily; in the morning before you leave home and at night before going to bed. Find a comfortable grounded position before you start.

Grounding yourself before meditation

Sit in a comfortable meditative position. Whichever position you prefer, it is important that it is stable and balanced, and that you can hold it comfortably. Be sure that your knees are slightly lower than your pelvis. Do not lie down.

• **Sitting cross-legged** is the best position for stopping your energy from "leaking" and it facilitates your inward focus. It physically contains your energy, as your legs form a sort of infinity symbol. If you are having trouble lowering your knees, try raising your buttocks by sitting on a cushion or by placing a rolled-up blanket under your buttocks. Make sure that you don't sit up too high, otherwise your back will arch. Try to place your knees on the ground or else support them with cushions or rolled-up blankets.

• **Kneeling (vajrasana)** is the pose commonly used in Zen meditation. Sitting directly on your heels may be difficult; you may want to place a cushion or foam yoga block between your buttocks and heels. Alternatively, you could try using a kneeling bench. In this position, the front of your shins and feet are in contact with the ground. Make sure that your buttocks are resting firmly on your heels, cushion or bench.

• **Sitting on a chair** Use a straight-backed chair with a firm seat. Keep your body parallel to the chair's back and don't lean against it. Keep your feet flat on the floor and don't cross your ankles. If your knees are not slightly lower than your pelvis, place a cushion or yoga block under your buttocks. If your feet don't reach the floor, rest them firmly on a cushion or a block.

Support your knees and hips so that you can sit comfortably during meditation.

Sit up straight, but be relaxed about it. Posture strongly affects the state of your mind. If you slump forward, you will tend to fall asleep. Alternatively, if you sit up too straight and rigidly, you create tension in your body.

It is important to keep your back straight so that your energy can travel up your spine and your breath can be full. When your back is bent, the movements of your diaphragm and ribcage are impeded, making it difficult to breathe. When you can't take a full, deep breath, there is the tendency to fall asleep; or you may feel a little anxious, which is counter-productive when you are trying to ground yourself.

You may find it helpful to imagine a fine thread pulling your head up and another thread attached to the top of your breastbone, keeping your chest upright. Bring your hands into one of the grounding mudras. Mudras seal your prana into particular subtle channels; they also send a signal to your mind that helps to ground your body.

Jnana mudra is a good hand position to use in meditation and visualization practices. Join the tips of your thumb and forefinger on each hand. Then rest the inside of your wrists on the respective knees or thighs with your fingers pointing downward. Prithivi (earth) mudra may also be helpful; it is formed by joining the tip of each ring finger with the tip of the thumb on the same hand. The remaining fingers are relaxed and the inside of the wrists are placed on the respective knees or thighs, with your fingers pointing downward.

Grounding visualization

1. Think of the qualities of earth. Feel as though you are rooting yourself firmly, drawing stability and strength. Pay particular attention to the pull of gravity and its effects on your body.

2. Be aware of the parts of your body that are in contact with the ground (or your chair). Feel as though these parts are growing roots. See the roots going deep into the earth.

③ After a while, you will probably begin to experience a pleasant heaviness that becomes a feeling of stability and stillness.

Variation: You may also choose to do this grounding visualization while standing up, as in the exercise, "Standing on the earth with full awareness" (see page 88).

Diet

If you tend to feel spaced out and flighty, it is especially important to eat a diet that will help you to ground yourself. In ayurveda, people with vata (air) imbalance are encouraged to stay away from raw foods and instead eat nourishing, cooked foods, especially root vegetables and complex carbohydrates. So, eat more root vegetables. Roots have the job of stabilizing the plant, as well as taking in nourishment – and will do the same for you.

Eating is one of the best ways to create a short-term grounding. Eating heavy foods, in particular, can be very efficient, but be careful not to abuse the use of food. Proper grounding is best when it is the result of your mastery of energy.

If you choose to sit in a chair for meditation, make sure that your feet are firmly planted on the ground.

Cleansing

If you live in a city, work with other people, go to restaurants, use public transport or interact with others in a variety of ways, it is almost impossible to not pick up some negativity, at least occasionally. You might find it helpful to cleanse your chakra energy, letting go of negative emotions and thoughts.

The most common technique for cleansing, which you no doubt use already, is to wash your hands and shower frequently. Whenever you return from a public place, wash your hands then shake them vigorously for 10–20 seconds, but not in the direction of another person. Other techniques include:

• Remove all jewelry and your watch. Stretch your arms straight out in front of you. Rub each arm with the opposite hand in a sharp, brisk motion. Start at your shoulder and rub outward toward your hand – then do the other side. Repeat this five or six times on each side. This simple exercise is a quick cleanse of your aura and enables you to "let go" of recent negative energy that you might have inadvertently picked up.

• If you are in a place with cold running water, let the water run down each forearm in turn, starting from your inner elbow down to your hand. Let the water run for 30 seconds and then repeat on the other arm.

• Fill a sink or large bowl with cold water. Tie your hair back, if it is long. Place your forehead and the front part of your head in the water (you may prefer to keep your eyes closed, but it is not necessary) and hold for about one minute. Be sure to dry your hair properly afterwards. This cleanses your ajna and sahasrara chakras and also stimulates a cleansing response in your entire chakra system.

- Many people prefer to use a technique of visualizing light running through their chakras to clean, energize and balance them. To work with light, sit in a comfortable meditation position with your back straight. Ground yourself before you begin (see pages 264–7). Take a few slow, deep breaths down into your lower abdomen. Relaxing gently, imagine a beautiful white or golden light above your head. Feel the light entering your crown chakra (sahasrara); notice whether or not you experience any physical sensations. Slowly move the light down, chakra by chakra, until you reach your base chakra.

- You can also concentrate on cleansing each chakra separately before a meditation session. For example, if you feel you have some impurity in a certain chakra, you can cleanse that chakra by visualizing light running through it.

- Another technique is similar to the grounding exercise on page 266. As you visualized roots going down into the earth, remind yourself that roots have two jobs. They not only ground you; they can also take in nutrients and purify your energy. Feel as though you are drawing up pure cleansing energies from the earth.

A sharp downward motion on each arm can provide a quick cleanse of unwanted energies.

- Cleanse with physical light from a fire. In India, lights are waved and mantras chanted at the end of every meditation session. Then each person cups hands over the light and symbolically brings it over the body. You can do this using a candle: place your hands on either side of the flame and gently draw the light toward your being.

- Imagine a vortex of white light; you might like to visualize a tornado of white light whirling through each chakra, picking up debris and carrying it away.

- Take a salt bath or smudge by burning purifying herbs, such as sage, to cleanse your entire aura.

Burning sage provides an excellent herb purification of the environment.

CHAKRA	HOW TO PURIFY
Sahasrara	Sunlight; meditation; communion with the Divine
Ajna	Purify your mind by filling it with divine thoughts and prayer. Try to watch fewer violent films and TV programmes.
Vishuddha	Stop using toxic language. Cleanse through sound and mantra repetition. Make a conscious effort to always speak the truth – make sure that your words, thoughts and deeds are cohesive and authentic. Release blocks in your creative flow of energy. Give thanks before eating; express gratitude for blessings received in life.
Anahata	Cleanse through deep breathing (the element of air). Forgive those who you feel have injured you in some way. Forgive yourself for the mistakes you have made. Forgive, but do not forget; learn from your mistakes and move on. If you have deep-seated grief, do not cling to it. If your sorrow is more recent, grieve fully.
Manipura	Cleanse physically through exercises, such as yoga practice, as well as more active (fiery) activities such as running or dancing. Share food with friends. Purify your self-image by releasing disempowering thoughts. Release your anger by detaching yourself from it.
Swadhisthana	Use the element of water: fast on water; sweat and go to the sauna; practise hydrotherapy (warm baths containing mineral salts). Let go of guilt and shame.
Muladhara	Use food, as a manifestation of earth, to encourage elimination and detoxification. Eat lightly, but eat foods that will ground your energies. Increase your intake of fibre and purifying foods. Eat when physically hungry, but not to fill emotional needs. Release fear. Let go of negative family habits and behaviour patterns.

Addictions, Obsessions and Dangerous Substances

Addictions suppress spiritual growth by depleting or blocking the flow of your prana. They cloak your feelings by dulling your mind and making it heavy and lethargic. Their effect on your mind is to fill it with inertia and dejection, often making things appear other than they are in reality.

Obsessions tend to stimulate your mind to look elsewhere; they create false craving and restlessness in your mind. Because of these mental agitations, you may experience unreasonable desires, anger, envy, greed and jealousy.

Each addiction or obsession suppresses some form of emotional energy. The first step in removing addictions and obsessions is to free yourself from the need to suppress that particular emotion. Working with the energy of your chakras can enable you to find healthy ways of having a negative emotional surface, so that you can acknowledge and release it.

All addictions create scars in your psyche. They introduce toxins into your physical and astral bodies. Some can forcefully raise your consciousness, but this opening is transient, uncontrolled, completely unprotected and often distorted. Alcohol can present a danger if you consume it too close to working with your chakras. Alcohol forces your chakras to be too open and enhances your ability to absorb negative vibrations. Tranquillizers and anti-psychotic drugs also make it increasingly difficult for you to connect with the energy of your higher chakras, while heroin and other hard drugs are totally incompatible with chakra work. Even marijuana, which has been touted as having no negative physical side effects, can deaden the flow of your prana and weaken your nadis (subtle energy channels).

CHAKRA	COMMON ADDICTION	HIDDEN BY ADDICTION
Sahasrara	Cult behaviour, fundamentalist religions	Lack of authentic mystical experience
Ajna	Hallucinogens	Lack of authentic vision
	Marijuana	Sadness. Less communication between the ajna and other chakras, so your "great ideas" are not put into practice.
	Caffeine	Mental tiredness
Vishuddha	Opiates, marijuana	Inability to communicate
Anahata	White sugar	Not being loved
	Caffeine	Lack of empathy
	Chocolate	Loneliness, cravings for love
Manipura	Nicotine	Anger
	Caffeine	Inability to connect with others
	Overeating	Excessive sensitivity
	Amphetamines, cocaine, stimulants	Lack of energy
	Depressants	Excessive, uncontrolled energy
Swadhisthana	Sex, heroin, excitement, danger	Feeling stuck in life
	Shopping	Inner emptiness
	Alcohol	Lessening inhibitions
Muladhara	Gambling, shopping, work	Feelings of insecurity
	Overeating	Feeling ungrounded
	Alcohol	Fear

Samanu meditation to cleanse and ground

Sit in a comfortable cross-legged, meditative position. Join the tips of the thumb and index finger of your left hand. Rest the inside wrist of your left hand on your left knee, with your fingers pointing downward. This hand position, known as jnana mudra, helps you to steady your mind and ground your energy.

Raise your right hand and fold the two fingers next to the thumb into your palm. This is vishnu mudra. During this exercise, you will be using the thumb of your right hand to close your right nostril and the two end fingers (ring and little fingers) to close your left nostril.

I Air purification

1 Close your right nostril with your right thumb. Inhale through your left nostril, mentally repeating the mantra of air "YAM". Inhale until you have comfortably filled your lungs. Focus on your heart chakra, the energy centre of the air element. Visualize air/wind flowing through your nadis, blowing away impurities.

2 As you finish the inhalation, gently pinch both nostrils closed. Hold your breath while mentally repeating the mantra "YAM". Be sure to keep your focus on the region of your heart.

3 Release the thumb from your right nostril. Exhale very

This exercise makes use of both your breath and mantras for purifying your physical and astral bodies.

slowly through the right nostril as you repeat the mantra "YAM". Let your attention remain focused on your heart chakra.

2 Fire purification

① Inhale through your right nostril, repeating "RAM", the mantra of fire, and focusing on your solar plexus region. Visualize fire as burning away all psychic, emotional and mental impurities.

② Close both nostrils and hold your breath as you mentally repeat the mantra "RAM".

③ Release your left nostril. Exhale slowly through the left nostril as you repeat "RAM" mentally. Your focus remains focused on the region of your manipura.

3 Divine nectar to wash away remaining impurities

① Inhale through your left nostril, repeating "TAM", mantra of the moon. Have your attention fixed on the minor chakra that is located just inside your left eyebrow.

② Close both nostrils and hold your breath while repeating "TAM". During retention, imagine that divine nectar from the moon centre is flowing through all of your nadis to cleanse and soothe them.

4 Grounding your energy

① Release your thumb from your right nostril and exhale slowly. Bring your attention to the base of your spine; mentally repeat "LAM", the mantra of the earth element.

② Release your nostrils. Lower your right hand and bring it into jnana mudra, resting on your right knee. Both hands are now in the same position with your fingers pointing downward. Sit silently for at least 10 minutes, with your full attention on your muladhara chakra. As you continue to mentally repeat the mantra "LAM", feel secure, fully present and aware of your connection with the earth.

Further Reading

Johari, Harish, *Chakras: Energy Centers of Transformation*, Destiny Books: Vermont, 2000

Judith, Anodea, *Eastern Body, Western Mind: Psychology and the Chakra System as a Path to the Self,* Celestial Arts: Berkeley, 2004

Leadbeater, C.W., *The Chakras*, Quest Books: Wheaton, 1972

Minish, Deana, *Chakra Foods for Optimum Health: A Guide to the Foods that Can Improve Your Energy, Inspire Creative Changes, Open Your Heart and Heal Body, Mind and Spirit,* Conari Press: San Francisco, 2009

Myss, Caroline, *Anatomy of the Spirit: The Seven Stages of Power and Healing*, Three Rivers Press: London, 1997

Northrup, Christiane, *Women's Bodies, Women's Wisdom: The Complete Guide to Women's Health and Wellbeing,* Piatkus Books: London, 1998

Saradananda, Swami, *Chakra Meditation: Discover Energy, Creativity, Focus, Love, Communication, Wisdom and Spirit*, Duncan Baird Publishers: London, 2008

Saradananda, Swami, *The Power of Breath: The Art of Breathing Well for Harmony, Happiness and Health*, Duncan Baird Publishers: London, 2009

Satyananda Saraswati, Swami, *Kundalini Tantra*, Yoga Publications Trust: Munger, Bihar, India, 2001

Vishnu-devananda, Swami, *Hatha Yoga Pradipika with Modern Commentary*, Om Lotus Publishing: New York, 1997

Woodroffe, Sir John (Arthur Avalon), *The Serpent Power: The Secrets of Tantric and Shaktic Yoga*, Dover Publications: New York, 1974

Glossary

A

Agni: (1) fire; element of manipura chakra; (2) Vedic fire god (deva), guardian of the manipura chakra

Airavata: mythological elephant with seven trunks; vehicle of Indra, the king of the devas (Vedic gods)

Ajna chakra: sixth from lowest chakra, located between the two eyebrows; the "third eye"

Akasha: space; ether. The element of the vishuddha (throat) chakra).

Anahata: (1) heart chakra; (2) mystical, soundless sound

Ananda: bliss, joy, infinite happiness

Apana: downward moving aspect of prana that enables you to let go of what you no longer need or want

Ardhineshwara: divine hermaphrodite; Siva and Shakti together in the same body

Asana: yoga posture, position, poses for meditation and/or body control

Ashram: place of spiritual retreat where one practises yoga

Ayurveda: traditional medicine of India

B

Bandha: muscular locks applied by yogis during certain breathing exercises

Bhagavad Gita: Indian scripture that deals with various aspects of yoga

Bhakti: devotion

Bija: seed; source

Bija mantra: one-syllable seed, core mantra

Bindu: concentrated energy; inner point of focus in a yantra

Brahma granthi: first and lowest psychic knot, located at the muladhara chakra

C

Chakra: psychic energy centre, located along the central meridian in the astral body

D

Dakini: feminine energy that governs the muladhara chakra

Darshan: insight; way of seeing; vision

Deva: god or angel; a celestial being

Devi: divinity in its female aspect; the Divine Mother Goddess

Dharma: Righteous conduct

G

Ganesha: elephant-headed god who is the remover of obstacles; the masculine guardian of the muladhara chakra

Granthi: energetic "knot" that acts as a protective mechanism to shield from excessive kundalini energy

Guna: quality or attribute; the three qualities of nature: sattva, rajas and tamas

Guru: spiritual teacher; one who removes darkness

H

Hanuman: monkey god symbolizing the prana

Hara point: region of the manipura chakra regarded as the centre of control and strength in the Taoist tradition

Hatha yoga: aspect of yoga that uses physical and breathing exercises to work with the prana

Hatha Yoga Pradipika: 16th-century hatha yoga scripture

I

Ida: one of the major meridians (nadi); situated to the left of the spine

Indra: king of the devas (Vedic gods), who rides on Airavata and is the guardian of the vishuddha (throat) chakra

J

Japa: repetition of mantra

K

Kakini: feminine energy that governs the anahata (heart) chakra

Karma: action; the law of action and reaction, or cause and effect

Karma yoga: selfless service

Kosha: sheath; layer

Kriya: yoga cleansing or purification exercise

Kundalini: potential psychic energy; primordial cosmic energy; from the word "kundala" meaning "coiled"

L

Lakini: feminine energy that governs the manipura chakra

Lingam: symbol of Siva; a form that represents the Formless Absolute

M

Makara: mythological crocodile with a fish's tail; vehicle of Ganga (the Ganges River)

Mandala: circular stylized design representing the universe; a visual tool for meditation

Manipura chakra: third from bottom chakra, located in the solar plexus region

Mantra: Sacred syllable, word or set of words used for meditation

Maya: the cosmic Illusion

Moksha: liberation from the bondage of karma, from the wheel of birth and death

Mouna: silence as a spiritual practice; voluntarily keeping silent in order to observe and quiet the mind

Mudra: (1) hatha yoga exercise that "seals" the prana; (2) hand gesture

Muladhara chakra: lowest centre of psychic energy, located at base of body

N

Nadi: astral nerve, psychic pathway; equivalent to the meridians of acupuncture

Namaskar: Indian gesture of greeting that consists in bringing the palms together in front of the heart, signifying "my soul meets your soul"

P

Pingala: one of the major meridians (nadi); situated to the right of the spine

Prana: (1) vital energy; chi; ki; (2) aspect of life force that enables you to take in things

Pranayama: yoga breathing exercises; control of prana

R

Rajas: one of the three essential qualities of nature; the quality of activity, passion, restlessness

Rakini: feminine energy that governs the swadhisthana chakra

Rudra granthi: top-most psychic knot in the sushumna, located at the ajna chakra

S

Sadhana: spiritual practice

Sahasrara chakra: Lotus of the Thousand Petals; the highest chakra

Samadhi: the super-conscious state

Samana: the aspect of prana that enables you to process (digest) what you take in (whether it is food, air or ideas)

Samsara: continuous wheel of birth and death

Sat-Cakra-Nirupana: ancient tantric text, translated with commentary in Sir John Woodroffe's book, *The Serpent Power*

Satsang: association with spiritually minded people; the company of wise people

Sattva: One of the three essential qualities of nature; the quality of purity and light

Shakini: feminine energy that governs the vishuddha (throat) chakra

Shakti: the active creative feminine principle of the universe

Shanti: Peace

Siva: pure consciousness; passive masculine principle; the eternal witness

Siva Samhita: ancient hatha yoga scripture

Sushumna: one of the major meridians (nadi); situated at the centre of the body, approximating the spine

Swadhisthana chakra: second from lowest chakra, located in the sacral region of the lower back

T

Tamas: One of the three essential qualities of nature; the quality (guna) of darkness, inertia and infatuation

Tamasic: Impure; rotten (with reference to food); lazy; dull

Tantra: yoga practice laying emphasis on repetition of mantras and other esoteric meditations

U

Udana: aspect of prana that directs your aspirations upward and aids in the production of the voice

V

Varuna: Vedic water god; masculine guardian of the swadhisthana chakra

Vata: ayurvedic bodily constitution that is symbolized by the wind element

Vayu: wind, air; the element of the anahata (heart) chakra

Vishnu granthi: the second knot in the sushumna, located at the anahata chakra

Visuddha chakra: fifth from lowest chakra, located at the throat

Vyana: aspect of prana that circulates energy

Y

Yakini: feminine energy that governs the sahasrara chakra

Yantra: stylized diagram that is used as a meditation tool

Yoga Sutra: ancient yoga scripture compiled by the sage Patanjali

Index

acupuncture 13, 14, 30
addictions 272–5
affirmations: ajna chakra 204
anahata chakra 160
  manipura chakra 138
  muladhara chakra 92
  swadhisthana chakra 116
  vishuddha chakra 182
African traditions 20
air 18, 19, 146, 250
air purification 274–5
ajna chakra 9, 188–209
  addictions and 273
  balancing ajna energy 200–1
  benefits 190
  cleansing 268, 271
  drawing 71
  granthis 28
  healing functions 190
  imbalances 198–9
  intellectual blockages 46, 49
  journaling 193
  meditations 19, 196, 204–5
  relationships 202–3, 224, 225
  relationships with other chakras 168, 235, 238, 240–1, 243, 246–7, 249

symbolic element and energy 20, 194–5, 250
using 192–3
when to work with ajna energy 193
working with 206–9
akido 140
alternative nostril breathing 39, 40–1
anahata chakra 9, 144–65
  addictions and 273
  balancing anahata energy 156
  benefits 146
  cleansing 271
  drawing 71
  granthis 28
  healing functions 146
  imbalances 154–5
  journaling 148
  meditations 19, 152–3, 160–1
  relationships 115, 158–9, 224, 225
  relationships with other chakras 181, 234, 237–8, 242–3, 247, 249
  symbolic element and energy 150–1
  using 148–9
  when to work with 148
  working with 162–5
anger 42

Anthroposophy 22
ardha-chandrasana 228–30
ardha-matsyendrasana 140–2
ardho-mukhshwanasana 94–5
asanas 35, 36, 38
astral body 10–13, 26, 28, 31
aura 13, 38, 258, 268
Avalon, Arthur 22
awkward twist, seated 142–3
ayurveda 264, 267

badha-konasana 118–19
balance: ajna chakra 198, 200–1
  anahata chakra 156
  manipura chakra 134–5
  muladhara chakra 88–9
  sahasrara chakra 222–3
  wadhisthana chakra 112–13
  vishuddha chakra 178–9
balasana 94–5
bandhas 26, 30–1
baths, energy-cleansing 112–13
bhrumadhya drishti 208–9
bhuchari 204–5
bindu 59

bio-magnetic field 13, 38, 258
blockages: energetic 38–41
  intellectual 46–9
  karmic 50–3
  mental-emotional 42–5
  physical 34–7
Bonpo religion 20
bound-angle pose 118–19
bow pose 164–5
Brahman 226
breathing exercises 26, 30, 178–9, 182–3
  alternative nostril breathing 39, 40
  pranayama 24, 35, 36, 39–41, 45
the bridge 120–1
brow chakra see ajna chakra
Buddhism 226

camel pose 162–4
causal body 10–13
chair pose 97–8
chakras 8–9
  benefits of working with 16–17
  clothing for chakra work 258
  drawing 70–1
  energy centres 14
  expanding and contracting 260–2
  inter-relationships 232–53

mantras and 61
meditations to prepare for 72–5
opening and closing 256, 260–3
protection during 256–63
releasing blockages 34–53
sources of chakra wisdom 18–19
in the Western world 22–3
working with 19
see also individual chakras
chakrasana 164–5
chandrasana 118–20
Cherokee traditions 20
chi 13, 20
child's pose 94–5
Chinese medicine 140
chitta 212
Christianity 20, 23
cleansing 268–71
  meditation and 274
clothing, for meditation and chakra work 258
communication skills: ajna chakra 203
  through the chakras 224–5
  vishuddha chakra 170, 180
connections, instinctive 91
consciousness 10
cow's head pose 164–5

cross-legged pose, sitting 265
crown chakra see sahasrara chakra

dangerous substances 272–5
depression 42–3
devotional practices 45
dhanruasana 164–5
diaries, practice 64–7
  see also journaling
diet 35, 36, 267
divine nectar to wash away remaining impurities 275
dog poses: downward-facing dog pose 94–6
  upward-facing dog pose 162–3
doubt 46
downward-facing dog pose 94–6
dreamwork 193, 201
drugs 272

earth 18, 19, 250
Egyptian traditions 20
elements 18
  ajna chakra 194–5
  anahata chakra 150–1
  manipura chakra 128–9
  meditation on the inter-relationship between 250–3
  muladhara chakra 82–3
  sahasrara chakra 216–17

swadhisthana chakra
106–7
vishuddha chakra
172–3
emotional blockages
42–5
energy: benefits of
chakra work 16–17
energetic blockages
38–40
energy centres 14
energy-cleansing baths
112–13
granthis 28
kundalini 24–7, 28, 30
mudras and bandhas
30–1
and relationships 71
releasing blockages
34–53
yantras 56–9
see also individual
chakras
essential oils 112
ether 18, 19, 250
etheric double 13, 38
expansiveness meditation
72–3

fasting 36, 45, 134–5
fault-finding 46
fear 43–4
fire 18, 19, 124, 250
fish pose 120–1
forgiving 148
forward bends: single-
legged forward bends
118–19

standing forward bend
96–7
freeing 18, 19
frontal gaze 208–9
fullness 226

gaze into the void 204–5
goddess squat 120–1
gomukhasana 164–5
granthis 28
Greek mythology 20
grounding 88, 264–7
cleansing and 269
grounding your energy
275
meditation and 264–5,
274
and muladhara chakra
90, 91, 248
visualizations 264, 266
working with chakras
18, 19
gut feelings 137, 240

hakini mudra 200–1
half-moon pose 228–30
half-spinal twist 140–2
hand gestures 200–1
hara point 136, 140,
240
hatha yoga 20
headstand 206–8
healing functions: ajna
chakra 190
nahata chakra 146
manipura chakra 124
muladhara chakra 78
sahasrara chakra 212

swadhisthana chakra
102
vishuddha chakra 168
heart chakra see anahata
chakra
Hermes 20
high namaskar 228–9
Higher Self 214, 216
holodynamic breathing
26
humming breath 178–9

imbalances: ajna chakra
198–9
anahata chakra 154–5
manipura chakra
132–3
muladhara chakra 86–7
sahasrara chakra 220–1
swadhisthana chakra
110–11
vishuddha chakra
176–7
Inca traditions 20
infinite consciousness
212
intellectual blockages
46–9
intellectual pride, letting
go 48

janu-sirshasana 118–19
jathara parivritti 140–1
Johari, Harish 23
journaling 52, 64–5
ajna chakra 193
anahata chakra 148
manipura chakra 127

muladhara chakra 81
practice diaries 66–7
sahasrara chakra 215
swadhisthana chakra 105
vishuddha chakra 171
Judith, Anodea 23
juice fasting 134–5
Jung, Carl 23

Kabbalah 20, 23
kalikasana 120–1
karmic blockages 50–3
ki 13, 20
kindness, acts of 51
kneeling (vajrasana) 265
kneeling crescent moon 118–20
knots, psychic 28
Krishna, Gopi 23
kriya 35, 36
kundalini 8, 24–7, 82
   and the granthis 28
   kundalini yoga 23
   mudras and 30
   and muladhara chakra 248
   sensations of awakening 27

lake, visualizing your mind as a 116–17
language 202
layers of being, meditation on 74–5
Leadbeater, C. W. 22–3
letting go 158–9
life force 13

the lion 184–6
Locus Mundi 59
lotus mudra 156–7
loving-kindness meditation 160–1

manipura chakra 9, 122–43
   addictions and 273
   balancing 134–5
   benefits of 124
   blockages 42
   leansing 271
   drawing 71
   healing functions 124
   imbalances 132–3
   journaling 127
   meditations 19, 130–1, 138–9
   relationships 136–7, 225
   relationships with other chakras 181, 234, 237, 240–1, 242–3, 247, 249
   using 126–7
   when to work with 126
   working with 140–3
mantras 26, 60–3, 182–3
   ajna chakra 194
   anahata chakra 150
   manipura chakra 128
   muladhara chakra 82–3
   sahasrara chakra 216
   swadhisthana chakra 106
   vishuddha chakra 172

martial arts 13, 140
matsyasana 120–1
Mayan religion 20
meditation: ajna chakra 196, 204–5
   anahata chakra 152–3 160–1
   and cleansing 269
   closing your chakras after 262
   clothing for 258
   on Divine Light 226–7
   expansiveness meditation 72–3
   grounding for 264–5
   on inter-relationship of the elements 250–3
   on layers of being 74–5
   on letting go 48–9
   manipura chakra 130–1, 138–9
   muladhara chakra 84–5, 92–3
   perceiving your weaknesses and strengths 68–9
   to prepare for chakra work 72–5
   sahasrara chakra 226–7
   to strengthen the sacral–heart connection 239
   samanu 274
   swadhisthana chakra 108, 116–17
   to transform anger 42, 138–9

vishuddha chakra
182–3
and visualizing
elements 19
yantras as 56–9
mental blockages 42–5
mental bodies 30
Mercury 20
meridians see nadis
mind 18
mind's eye see third eye
mouna 38
mudras 26, 30, 156,
200–1, 266, 274
muladhara chakra 9,
76–99
addictions and 273
balancing energy 88–9
benefits 78
blockages at your 43
cleansing 271
drawing 71
grounding and 264
healing functions 78
imbalances 86–7
journaling 81
and kundalini 24
meditations 19, 84–5,
92–3, 250
relationships 90–1
relationships with
other chakras 137,
234–5, 236, 242,
246, 248
symbolic elements and
energy 82–3
using 80–1
when to work with 81

working with 94–9
music 45
Myss, Caroline 23

nadanusandhana 222–3
nadis 10, 13, 14
addictions and 272
ajna chakra 190
and awakening
kundalini 24, 28
releasing blockages
34–53
sahasrara chakra 212
in Taoist teachings 20
namaskar 162–3,
228–9
nasagra drishti 208–9
nasal gaze 208–9
Native American
traditions 20
neck stretches 185–7
negativity 46, 48
letting go of 148
nervous system 13, 42
neti 36, 37

obsessions 272–5
OM 62, 222–3

padagushtasana 96–7
parivritta trikonasana
142–3
parivritta utkatasana
142–3
physical body 10–13,
74–5
composition of 18
prana flow and 38, 45

purification and 26,
30, 31
poorna 226
positive thinking 49
prana 10, 13
addictions and 272
asanas 38
blockages and 38, 43
expansiveness
meditations 72–3
granthis 28
mudras 30
releasing blockages
34–53
in Taoist teachings 20
pranayama 24, 35, 36,
39–41, 45
pranic sheath 38
prayer position 162–3
pre-conceived ideas 44
protection, during
energetic work
256–63
psychic abilities 48, 193
psychic sponges 56
psychic vampires 257
purification: air 274–5
fire 275
see also cleansing
Purnananda 22

qigong 140

rebirthing 26
reclining abdominal twist
140–1
reflection, aids to 64–9
reflexology 13

relationships: ajna chakra 202–3
anahata chakra 158–9
between the chakras 232–53
energetic 71
manipura chakra 136–7
muladhara chakra 90–1
sahasrara chakra 224–5
swadhisthana chakra 114–15
vishuddha chakra 180–1
Roman mythology 20
root chakra see muladhara chakra
rotated triangle 142–3
rudra granthi 28

sacral chakra see swadhisthana chakra
sacral-heart connection, meditation to strengthen 239
sacred geometry 56–7
sahasrara chakra 9, 210–31
addictions and 273
balancing sahasrara energy 222–3
benefits 212
cleansing 268, 271
drawing 71
energy 221
healing functions 212
imbalances 220–1
journaling 215
meditations 19, 218, 226–7, 250
relationships 224–5
relationships with other chakras 235, 238, 243, 247, 248–9
sahasrara yantra 218
symbolic element and energy 216–17
using 214–15
when to work with 215
working with 228–31
samanu meditation 274
sarvangasana 184–5
satchidananda 212
scorpion pose 230–1
seed body 10–13
self, sense of 124
self-doubt 46
self-esteem 132, 137
self-expression, suppression of 181
self-less service 51
sethu-bandhasana 120–1
shiatsu 13
shoulderstand 184–5, 313
shunya 226
simhasana 184–6
single-legged forward bend 118–19
sirsasana 206–8
sitting on a chair pose 265–6
sixth sense 190
SO HAM meditation

listening to the sound of your breath 182–3
solar plexus chakra see manipura chakra
sorrow 158
sound, mantras and 60–3
speech 176
standing on the earth with full awareness exercise 88–9, 267
standing forward bend 96–7
Steiner, Rudolf 22
strengths, perceiving 68–9
subtle body 14, 38, 146, 168, 190
subtle-energy leeching 137
swadhisthana chakra 9, 43, 100–21
addictions and 273
balancing 112–13
benefits 102
cleansing 271
drawing 71
healing functions 102
imbalances 110–11
journaling 105
meditations 19, 108, 116–17, 250
relationships 114–15, 224, 225
relationships with other chakras 234, 236–9, 241, 242, 244–5, 246–7, 249

symbolic element and
    energy 106–7
using 104–5
when to work with 105
working with 118–21
symbolism: ajna chakra
    194–5
anahata chakra 150–1
manipura chakra 128–9
muladhara chakra 82–3
sahasrara chakra
    216–17
swadhisthana chakra
    106–7
vishuddha chakra
    172–3

tai chi 140
Taoism 20, 136, 140
Taoist thyroid-
    strengthener 186–7
telepathic
    communication 202
Theosophical Society 23
third eye 190, 198, 240,
    246
thoughts, and effect on
    prana flow 45
three bodies 10–13
throat chakra see
    vishuddha chakra
thunderbolt pose 94–5
thyroid-strengthener,
    Taoist 186–7
Tree of Life 20, 23
tree pose 98–9
triangle pose 96–7
trikonasana 96–7

upward-facing dog pose
    162–3
urdhva-mukhaswanasana
    162–3
ustrasana 162–4
utkatasana 97–8

vajrasana 94–5, 265
vata 264, 267
viradhadrasana 98–9
vishnu granthi 28
vishuddha chakra 9,
    166–87
  addictions and 273
  balancing vishuddha
    energy 178–9
  benefits 168
  cleansing 271
  drawing 71
  healing functions 168
  imbalances 176–7
  intellectual blockages
    46
  journaling 171
  meditation 174, 182–3,
    250
  relationships 19, 180–1,
    224, 225
  relationships with
    other chakras 137,
    159, 203, 234–5,
    238, 241, 243,
    244–5, 247, 249
  symbolic element and
    energy 172–3
  when to work with 171
  working with 170–1,
    184–7

visualizations, grounding
    264, 266
vital energy 13
vocalization exercises 62
void (shunya) 226
vrikshasana 98–9
vrischikasana 230–1

walking meditation 92
warrior pose 98–9
water 18, 19, 102, 112,
    250
weaknesses, perceiving
    68–9
wheel pose 164–5
will-power 132
wisdom, sources of
    chakra 18–19
Woodroffe, Sir John 22

Yakini 217
yantras 56–9
  sahasrara yantra 218
  swadhisthana chakra
    108
yoga: and energetic
    blockages 38–9
  karma yoga 48
  yoga philosophy 10–11,
    18
  see also individual
    poses

Zen meditation 265

Acknowledgments

Picture Credits The publisher would like to thank the following people, museums and photographic libraries for permission to reproduce their material. Every care has been taken to trace copyright holders. However, if we have omitted anyone we apologize and will, if informed, make corrections to any future edition.

Page 6 Topfoto/© 2003 Charles Walker; **12** From "Subtle Body: Essence and Shadow" by David V. Tansley, Thames & Hudson Ltd, London; **15** Bridgeman Art Library/Private Collection/Archives Charmet; **17** Alamy/Cultura; **21** Art Archive/British Library; **22** Alamy/ Mary Evans Picture Library; **23** Art Archive/Culver Pictures; **25** Alamy/Bottle Brush; **26** Topfoto/© 2005 Charles Walker; **32** Pepin Press/Agile Rabbit Editions; **35** Alamy/Emil Pozar; **43** iStock/© Sergey Borisov; **44** iStock/© Ina Peters; **47** Wellcome Library, London. Wellcome Images; **51** Corbis/Frédéric Soltan; **054** Pepin Press/Agile Rabbit Editions; **061** Photolibrary.com/Still Pictures/Philippe Hays; **063** SuperStock/Somos Images; **065** Photolibrary.com/Blend Images/Jose Luis Pelaez Inc; **079** Bridgeman Art Library/ Museum of Fine Arts, Boston, Massachusetts. John H. and Ernestine A. Payne Fund, Helen S. Coolidge Fund, Asiatic Curator's, John W. Willard & Marshall H. Gould Funds; **080** Shutterstock/© XuRa; **083** Dreamstime/© Beholdereye; **090** Shutterstock/© Valua Vitaly ; **103** Alamy/ Stock Connection Distribution/Phoebe Dunn; **104** Bridgeman Art Library/ Bibliotheque Nationale, Paris, France/Archives Charmet; **107** Dreamstime/© Beholdereye; **113** Photolibrary.com/Emotive Images; **114** Shutterstock/© auremar; **125** Getty Images/ Brand X; **127** ©V&A Images – All rights reserved; **129** Dreamstime/© Beholdereye; **134** Shutterstock/© Goodluz; **147** Bridgeman Art Library/The Stapleton Collection; **149** Alamy/ Fancy; **151** Dreamstime/© Beholdereye; **169** Akg-images/Monique Pietri; **170** Alamy/ Imageshop; **173** Dreamstime/© Beholdereye; **180** iStock/© Kristian Sekulic; **191** Alamy/V&A Images; **192** Alamy/Louise Batalla Duran; **195** Dreamstime/© Beholdereye; **202** Alamy/MBI; **213** Alamy/Chris Selby; **214** Alamy/Westend61 GmbH/ Hans Huber; **217** Dreamstime/© Beholdereye; **232** Pepin Press/Agile Rabbit Editions; **237** Dreamstime/© Beholdereye; **247** Dreamstime/© Beholdereye; **251** Wellcome Library, London. Wellcome Images; **254** Pepin Press/Agile Rabbit Editions; **257** iStock/© Andreas Kermann; **270** Getty Images/Botanica/ Simon Watson

Author Acknowledgments
Swami Saradananda would like to thank Dr. Shelly Warwick, Director of the Touro-Harlem Medical Library in New York City, for her support and ability to shed new light on a variety of subjects.

Swami Saradananda can be contacted via her website: www.FlyingMountainYoga.org

Publisher's Acknowledgements
The publisher would like to thank:
Model: Sarina
Make-up artist: Justine Martin